YAR

Jane Eyre
CHARLOTTE BRONTË

Guide written by
Stewart Martin

A *Letts* *EXPLORE* Literature Guide

First published 1994
Reprinted 1994,1996, 1998, 2000
This edition revised by Ron Simps

Letts Educational
Aldine House
Aldine Place
London W12 8AW
020 8740 2266

Text © John Mahoney and Stewart Martin 1994

Self-test questions devised by Claire Wright

Typeset by Jordan Publishing Design

Text design Jonathan Barnard

Text illustrations Hugh Marshall

Cover illustration Ivan Allen

Design © Letts Educational Ltd

Acknowledgements
Outline answers are solely the responsibility of the author, and are not supplied or approved by the Exam Board.

British Library Cataloguing in Publication Data
A CIP record for this book is available from the British Library

ISBN 1 85758 254 3

Printed and bound in Great Britain

Ashford Colour Press, Gosport, Hampshire

Letts Educational Ltd, a division of Granada Learning Ltd. Part of the Granada Media Group.

www.letts-education.com

Contents

Plot synopsis   4

Who's who in *Jane Eyre*   5

Themes in *Jane Eyre*   8

Text commentary Chapters 1–15 (Volume 1)   13

Self-test questions Chapters 1–15 (Volume 1)   30

Text commentary Chapters 16–26 (Volume 2)   31

Self-test questions Chapters 16–26 (Volume 2)   43

Text commentary Chapters 27–38 (Volume 3)   45

Self-test questions Chapters 27–38 (Volume 3)   58

How to write a coursework essay   60

How to write an examination essay   65

Self-test answers   67

■ Plot synopsis

The story mainly takes place in three different locations in northern England – probably Northumberland, the West Riding and Derbyshire – and is set against the background of the 19th century class-system. Jane Eyre is an orphan child who lives with her uncle's family in Gateshead. After his death, his wife, Mrs Reed, mistreats Jane and eventually sends her away to Lowood, a school for orphans run by Mr Brocklehurst, a cruel man who starves the school's pupils and treats them badly. One of Jane's teachers, Miss Temple, is kind to her. Jane finds a friend in Helen Burns, but Helen falls ill and eventually dies in Jane's arms. An outbreak of typhus kills many of the pupils and brings the poor conditions at the school to public notice. The power of Mr Brocklehurst is reduced because of this, and conditions at the school improve.

Jane eventually becomes a teacher at the school but when Miss Temple marries and leaves, she feels it is also time for her to look to her own future. She gets a job as governess at Thornfield Hall and meets Mr Rochester. It soon becomes clear that he has a mysterious past. Strange events occur in the house, including an attempt to kill Rochester by setting fire to his bed. Jane falls in love with Rochester, who asks her to marry him. Just as they are about to be married, Mr Mason, a stranger from Rochester's past, announces that Rochester is already married. Rochester shows everyone his mad wife, Bertha, who has been kept locked up at Thornfield Hall.

Jane decides to leave. After wandering through the countryside and almost starving to death, she begs food at Moor House, the home of St John Rivers, the parson at Morton. He takes her in, and Jane and his sisters become friends. Jane takes a job as the village schoolmistress. St John begins increasingly to dominate her life, and eventually asks her to go with him as his wife to India, where he wants to be a missionary. She refuses, after hearing Rochester's voice calling to her inside her head. She returns to Thornfield to find that it has been burnt down by Rochester's wife, who has killed herself by jumping from the burning roof. She seeks out Rochester, who was blinded and crippled in the fire, and takes care of him at Ferndean house. They are married and Rochester's sight is partially restored.

■ Who's who in *Jane Eyre*

Jane Eyre

Jane is small and plain and these factors have a strong influence on her character and behaviour. Believing that she is unloved because of her plainness, she develops her wit and spirit in order to be noticed. She is intelligent and plain-spoken, strong-principled and self-willed. Her personality leads her into trouble at Gateshead. At Lowood she learns to control her feelings but they remain beneath the surface. At Thornfield her feelings blossom as adult love, but again she has to rein them in. Only at Moor House does she come to terms with her own feelings and this finally enables her to be fully herself at Ferndean.

Helen Burns

Helen is a symbol of Christian goodness in the book. She is patient, long-suffering and always ready to admit her own faults. She is serious, studious and philosophical about injustice. Helen acts as a counterbalance to Jane, who is more emotional and less disciplined. Jane learns self-control from Helen. Helen faces her death calmly and serenely because she is certain she is going to a better life.

Mr Rochester

Mr Rochester is a powerful, romantic character who is attractive without being handsome. A lively person who loves company, he is very witty but also has moods and an air of mystery. He turns out in the end to be loving, tolerant and passionate. He is seeking for goodness and finds it in Jane. He has a difficult struggle with himself before deciding to break the law and marry Jane, while his wife Bertha is still alive. He shows compassion towards Bertha but too much self-pity about his own circumstances. During the fire at Thornfield he loses an eye and a hand. This makes him a less arrogant and more humble man who is more able to live on equal terms with Jane, when she returns to him.

Mrs Reed

Mrs Reed is an unpleasant woman who is cruel towards Jane out of jealousy. Mrs Reed has some weaknesses in her character and Jane is able to get the better of her before she leaves Gateshead. Her premature death is caused by fear of poverty brought about by the extravagance then suicide of her wayward son. Before she dies she summons Jane to repair the wrongs that she has done her, but they do not make friends and she dies still unforgiving.

Miss Temple

Miss Temple is a kindly and fair-minded teacher who treats the girls at Lowood with respect and justice. She sorts out the matter of Jane's public disgrace by finding out the truth from Mr. Lloyd. She is admired because she practises what she preaches – unlike Mr Brocklehurst. Miss Temple has a special affection for Helen Burns and is the strongest influence on Jane while she is at Lowood.

St John Rivers

St John is a handsome man who is also very reserved. Although kind and dutiful, he is impatient with his present way of life. He says his ambition is to serve God as a missionary, but it seems as though he may be really serving his own ego. He holds his feelings under very strong control. Even though he admits to being very attracted to Rosamond Oliver, he does nothing about it, because she does not fit into his plans to serve God. St John has enormous influence over Jane, who is in awe of his unbending Christian righteousness.

Eliza and Georgiana Reed

Eliza is a greedy, miserly and calculating child. She grows up into a narrow-minded woman. She is preoccupied with religion and with her own routine. When her mother dies, she leaves home to become a nun. In some ways she is the female equivalent of St John Rivers.

Georgiana is just as self-centred as her sister Eliza, but is concerned only about her social life and her physical appearance. Like her sister, she lacks affection for her mother and uses Jane for her own ends. As a pair of sisters Eliza and Georgiana form a striking contrast to the affectionate, amiable and book-loving Diana and Mary Rivers. The unpleasant Reed family is completed by John, a weak, spoilt bully who eventually commits suicide.

Mr Brocklehurst

Mr Brocklehurst is a tall, grim-faced man who imposes harsh discipline at Lowood School. His religious teaching concentrates on sin and obedience rather than on love and tolerance. The pupils at Lowood freeze and starve because he thinks it is good for their souls.

Mrs Fairfax

Mrs Fairfax is the efficient housekeeper of Thornfield. She is friendly to Jane and treats her as an equal. She has a conventional outlook and lacks wit and humour. Because of this, she warns Jane against marrying Mr Rochester, thinking there is too much social difference between them.

Blanche Ingram

Blanche is a confident and accomplished woman who tries to court Mr Rochester but has no real affection for him – all she wants is his money and the social position that marrying him would bring. She is very self-centred and snobbish and treats Jane scornfully because she thinks a governess is not a very important person.

Bertha Rochester

She is an exaggerated character, typical of Gothic fiction, who is described as a violent, screaming woman with tangled black hair. She tries to kill Rochester and is responsible for the destruction of Thornfield.

Themes and images in *Jane Eyre*

Themes are the important ideas that run through the novel. You will come across them many times. They connect the story, the characters and the different parts of the plot.

When words and descriptions suggest a picture in your mind, this is called an **image**. Images are often used to make an idea stronger, or to encourage you to think of things from a particular point of view. If you described someone as being 'as thin as a rake', or as behaving 'like a wild animal', you would be using simple examples of images.

Many of the examples you will find are very striking and impressive. Other examples will be less obvious, so you will need to pay careful attention to the language that Charlotte Brontë uses. Read the following notes carefully.

Appearances

Appearances

Throughout the novel Brontë explores the difference between what seems to be real, and what is actually real. For example, she uses the way people dress to show how this plays a large part in determining how other people see them. She also shows how physical beauty can be a great asset in society. The novel sometimes uses the idea of appearances in a dramatic way.

A good example of this is the way Brontë uses mirrors. Mirrors can symbolise the contrast between reality and appearance. Brontë neither suggests that mirrors show us things the way they really are, nor that they necessarily distort things. Rather, she suggests that things seen in ordinary mirrors are subtly reversed. For instance, Brontë uses the idea to suggest the reflection – or contrast – between different characters. St John is a kind of mirror-image of Mr Rochester; Blanche Ingram is in the same way a reflection of Jane; Mr Brocklehurst is an echo of Miss Temple. This idea of reversal or opposites is also used when Brontë uses images connected with darkness and light to symbolise goodness and despair.

Birds

Birds

Descriptions of birds are frequent in the novel. References to them are always used very carefully, especially when describing Jane and Mr Rochester. Look at the way Brontë uses references to birdsong, the flight of birds and their appearance as ways of encouraging a particular response.

Books

Books

Throughout the novel, books are used as symbols of inspiration and comfort. They help to show the contrast between Jane and Helen. References to books underline the way imagination is seen as a means of escape from reality, offering refuge and shelter from a hostile world.

Social class

Social class

The story is set against the background of nineteenth-century society. Certain aspects of life at this time are emphasised in the book, especially attitudes towards poor relations, education, marriage and money. In particular, the role of education is fundamental to the development of the story. Three different aspects of education appear in the book: Lowood School, a charity boarding school for girls; Adèle's education by a governess; and a small village elementary school. Each of these episodes is used both to develop the plot and to reveal something about the characters involved. The references to schooling also show the progress of Jane's own education.

Dreams

Dreams

Dreams play an important part in the structure of the book because of where they appear in the action of the story. What the dreams reveal about the future adds to the feeling of suspense, which is an important feature of *Jane Eyre*'s structure.

Environment

Environment

Very often in the book you will find a vital link between the mood of a character and that of a scene or its surroundings. These links include references to the weather, the seasons and the countryside. This way of writing was common in nineteenth-century Gothic and Romantic literature, especially in poetry. The technical expression for this way of writing is 'pathetic fallacy'.

This means the error or false conclusion ('fallacy') of ascribing feelings ('pathetic' means something closer to the modern 'sympathetic') to inanimate objects. For example, in *Jane Eyre* Brontë uses descriptions of the wind, not only to suggest wild surroundings or storms, but also to represent mental agitation in some of the characters. It is as though the world of nature had 'moods' like a real person, and that these moods could be roused in sympathetic response.

Independence

Independence

The importance of independence is one of the main themes of the book. 'Independence' concerns the need for people to be faithful to themselves and their own natures and to develop as individuals in their own right. The conflicts that this can cause are explored in the story – conflicts with family, with authority, with religion and with social customs.

Linked with the theme of independence is a strong plea for a very modern idea – the right of women to equality. The emphasis is not so much on the need for equality of social opportunity – although regret is expressed at the narrowness of the choices available to women – but more on the importance of equality in personal relationships. Through the developing relationship between Jane and Mr Rochester, you see that it is possible for a man and a woman to have a relationship based on love, mutual respect, support and understanding, without either of them having to be dominant or subservient.

The themes of independence, equality and nature dominate the sections of the book set in Gateshead and Lowood, where they are explored through the injustices that take place there. A contrast is drawn between the different attitudes towards injustice shown by Jane and Helen, and what this tells you about their characters. In the same way, but much later on in the book, the themes of independence and rebellion appear at the same time as references to slavery and injustice. A good example of this is the description of the relationship between Jane and St John Rivers.

The theme of independence appears again during both of Jane's close relationships with men. Notice, for example, how the wedding acts both as a dramatic device in the story and as a symbol of control in the relationship between Jane and Mr Rochester. The occasion when the mad Bertha Rochester tears up the veil in Jane's bedchamber is a powerful and complex example of the way the themes of independence, control, slavery, rebellion and love interact throughout the story – in this particular case they are all present in Bertha's actions.

Having money is also a part of the theme of independence but its importance in Jane's life is not great and its value is not exaggerated. It is not as important as Jane's continual need to rebel. The importance of money serves as a background to the main concerns of the book, which are to do with the struggles that arise as Jane and other characters try to free themselves from the restraints they feel around them. Connected with this is Charlotte Brontë's treatment of religious and social hypocrisy. This is highlighted by contrasts – Mr Brocklehurst is an example of religious hypocrisy, while Miss Ingram is an example of social hypocrisy. Miss Temple and Jane herself are also used to contrast with the hypocrites around them.

Love and passion

Love and passion

One of the major themes of the novel is the desire to love and be loved. The story emphasises how important it is for people to be loved, and how lonely and isolated Jane feels when she is without friends. One of the driving forces in Jane's life is her desire for friendship, respect, affection and romantic love. This is shown in stark contrast to the search for other things – social position, money, God, etc. – which drives some of the other characters.

Passion is the word used here to describe the strength of feeling between Jane and Mr Rochester. The struggle between passion and control dominates the middle section of the book. Although this struggle is linked to the theme of nature, and the argument about nature and principle, it relates especially to Jane, whose need for emotional control is due to the social pressures that surround her.

Nature and character

Nature and character

One of the dominant themes of the book is the argument about how far people should behave according to their natural inclinations (their nature) and how far they should learn certain principles in order to control their nature. Some characters are examples of one side of the argument, whilst other characters illustrate the opposite side.

At Lowood you see the contrasting characters of Jane and Helen as examples of the two sides of this argument. Jane is torn between the two, but strives to free her own nature from the bonds surrounding her. At Thornfield, Jane decides to allow her principles to rule her nature and, when she is at Moor House, the argument between nature and principle is at its most stark.

Supernatural and spiritual

Supernatural and spiritual

The supernatural aspects of Jane Eyre are linked to other more general aspects of the novel's style. The novel has a strong Gothic flavour to it. 'Gothic' refers to the nineteenth-century taste for bloodcurdling, gruesome description, with special emphasis on strange wild creatures and vampires. Mary Shelley's *Frankenstein* is a good example of this kind of story. The supernatural and spiritual elements in *Jane Eyre* describe the 'other-worldly' sides of characters and events. This is most noticeable in the relationship between Jane and Mr Rochester, where it emphasises the spiritual nature of their love for each other, and also adds a touch of mystery to Mr Rochester's character. It is not used in any directly religious sense.

Essays/Examiner's tip icon

This icon is used to draw attention to a section of the **Text commentary** that is particularly relevant to either the section on **How to write a coursework essay** or to the section on **How to write an examination essay**. Each time it is used, a note identifies which section it relates to and adds a comment, quotation or piece of advice.

■ Text commentary

> *Jane Eyre* was originally published in three volumes. Most modern editions number the chapters straight through from 1 to 38, so this practice has been followed here. However, the **Self-test questions** have been placed at the end of Charlotte Brontë's original volumes, to remind you of its structure as a three-volume novel.

Chapter 1

Jane is living in her aunt's house at Gateshead. She is unloved and treated badly, but shows a determination to stand up for herself and fight for her independence.

'I was glad of it:...'

Although you are not aware of the nature of Jane's inferiority, notice how quickly she herself draws attention to it, showing that it plays on her mind.

Jane Eyre

Jane's isolated position in the Reed household is established in these opening paragraphs. You see at once that Mrs Reed does not like Jane, but that Jane is able to stand up for herself.

Brontë tells the story using a 'first-person narrator': events are described by – and from the point of view of – someone actually involved. The narrator here is, of course, Jane herself. This technique has several advantages. First, it engages our interest in the story and the main character, because we witness events through her eyes, and are aware of her thoughts and feelings. Secondly, the suspense is heightened, because we only know what the narrator herself knows: her uncertainty, hopes and fears are ours. Thirdly, it allows Brontë to switch perspectives: sometimes we see events as they are happening, while at others, we hear from the much older Jane at the time of writing.

'Folds of scarlet drapery...'

From her window-seat Jane watches the rain and wind outside. The opening paragraph of the book mentions 'clouds so sombre' and 'rain so penetrating' and this tells you about Jane's feelings and also serves to set the mood of the book.

Environment

Books play an important part in *Jane Eyre*. Jane's imagination is excited by the illustrations and writing in the book Bewick's *History of British Birds*. Jane finds many of the illustrations eerie and frightening.

'Each picture told a story;...'

Books

The servant Bessie is one of the few people who shows any interest in Jane when she was at Gateshead. Bessie plays an important role in feeding Jane's imagination with tales from popular books. Jane is reminded of events from these stories when she is in the red-room and describes her image in the mirror as 'half fairy – half imp'. Books and stories provide Jane with a way of escaping temporarily from her unhappy life at Gateshead.

' "Shew the book." '

Independence

One of the main themes of the novel is the constant search for independence. Jane is frequently reminded of her dependent position in the Reed household. For example, when John finds Jane reading Bewick's *History of British Birds*, he makes a point of insisting that it is one of the family's books. By doing this, he emphasises that Jane is not regarded as one of the family by the others, thus reminding her of her inferior place at Gateshead.

' "Wicked and cruel boy!" I said'

Jane Eyre

Several times Jane's position is compared to that of a slave. Look at how Jane calls John a 'slave-driver'. This insult is all the more pointed because, at the time when the book was written, the slave trade had not long been abolished and slavery still existed in countries like the United States. Jane is surprised by her own outburst, because she believes that she has her feelings under control, but you can tell from the way she reacts to John's assault that she has briefly lost control of her temper. Notice that nobody else comes to Jane's defence, but that they all hold her completely to blame – thus underlining her complete isolation within the household.

Bertha/Antoinette

Wide Sargasso Sea echoes other elements of *Jane Eyre*, as well as telling the unknown story of Bertha. Both novels begin with the desperate fears of childhood, Antoinette seeking places of safety, unbalanced by the bullying and mockery of other children.

Chapter 2

Jane is locked in the red-room as a punishment. She begins to think about death and ghosts and becomes terrified. Mrs Reed rejects her fears and locks her back inside the room. Jane faints with terror.

' "Master! How is he my master?" '

The position of any poor relation in a middle-class nineteenth-century family

Social class

was often difficult. Frequently such people were given a home by others only out of a sense of duty, rather than because of any real affection for them. In return, the poor relation was expected to show gratitude, so you can see why Jane's defiant attitude is not well received. Even the servants are shocked by Jane's behaviour. In the servants' eyes, Jane is inferior even to them, because she does not earn her keep. Look at Bessie's comment '…you are less than a servant…'.

' "What we tell you, is for..." '

Bessie is always ready to support the family against Jane, although she is not unkind. She speaks to Jane 'in no harsh voice'. Miss Abbot, on the other hand, is not so sympathetic, as you will see when Jane begs to be let out of the red-room.

'This room was chill...'

Supernatural
and spiritual

Brontë creates an atmosphere of eeriness in the red-room. Notice how she builds upon the 'chill…silent…solemn' atmosphere by telling you that this was the room where Jane's uncle died. The image of the mirror suggests a feeling of unreality: 'all looked colder…'. Even Jane's reflection reminds her more of a 'spirit' than of her real self.

'I was a discord in Gateshead Hall;...'

Appearances

The importance of the need to love and be loved is a strong theme in the book. Jane decides that her unhappiness is the result of her inability to love the Reeds and their inability to love her. Look at the ways in which she suggests her character does not fit in with theirs. She makes a special point of the fact that Mrs Reed would probably have liked her more if she had been beautiful.

'A singular notion dawned upon me.'

Supernatural
and spiritual

Now you see the full force of Jane's imagination. She broods on her uncle's death and wonders if his troubled spirit will appear. Notice how the combination of this thought and the ghostly light shining on the wall provokes terror in Jane's mind.

' "What is all this?" '

Mrs Reed's behaviour here confirms Jane's belief that her aunt is unable to love her. Jane's terror is interpreted as a trick to get out of the room, and Mrs Reed shows no sympathy for her. Mrs Reed sees Jane as a troublesome, stubborn child and a dangerous liar.

Mrs Reed

Chapter 3

Jane's suffering in the red-room and her subsequent illness make Bessie more sympathetic towards her. The apothecary, Mr Lloyd, suggests Jane should be sent away to school and Mrs Reed agrees. Jane discovers some details of her family background from the servants.

'I felt an inexpressible relief,...'

Jane's inferior position is underlined by the arrival of an apothecary to attend to her. A proper doctor would have been sent for if Mrs Reed's own children had been ill. But Jane is glad that he has arrived because he is kind. Notice Brontë's use of the word 'darkness' to describe Jane's sorrow.

Independence   The incident of the red-room has changed Bessie's feelings towards Jane – she now seems to have more sympathy for her. Bessie criticises her employers, but she will stand up for them in front of outsiders. Notice how Bessie tells lies to Mr Lloyd, and consider why she does this.

'Bessie had been down...'

Jane's 'wretchedness of mind' after the red-room incident is shown in her attitude to the book she takes to read. Normally a book would be a source of comfort and imaginative delight to Jane, but now it merely reflects her misery.

Books

' "None belonging to your father?" '

Jane's answers to Mr Lloyd's questions show that she is naive and ignorant of life. Her experience of poverty is limited to her aunt's nasty comments about her relatives and to the few poor villagers she has seen. She

has no real picture of honest, decent, working people. Jane admits to herself that she does not feel 'heroic' enough to obtain her liberty, if it means leaving her own class behind. This shows how strong class divisions were in the nineteenth

Social class   century.

Class plays an important part in Jane's life and history. Jane's mother was disinherited because she 'married beneath herself'. Were it not for this, Jane would have had financial independence.

Chapter 4

After three months, Jane meets Mr Brocklehurst, director of Lowood School. Mrs Reed blackens her character but Jane challenges this and frightens her.

'Eliza and Georgiana, evidently acting...'

Love and passion

Jane's isolation from the others increases after the red-room incident.

Her desire to love and be loved and the importance of this idea throughout the book is emphasised by the telling sentence: 'Human beings must love something'. For want of something better to love, Jane transfers her affections onto her doll.

'It was the fifteenth of January...'

Eliza's grasping nature is illustrated by the revelation that she is not above

Nature and character

charging her own mother interest on the money left in her care! Look carefully at the description of the weather before Mr Brocklehurst's arrival. Brontë uses this to signal the likely tone of the forthcoming interview with him. Look at the language used to describe Mr Brocklehurst: 'black pillar', 'carved mask', 'capital', 'stony stranger', which tells you a lot about Jane's first impressions of the man.

' "What must you do to avoid it?" '

Jane gives Mr Brocklehurst a very logical answer to the question about avoiding hell. It is obviously not the answer he expected and shows that Jane's approach to religion was not pious. Look at how she shocks him with her comments about the psalms on the next page ('Psalms are not interesting...').

' "I should wish her to be brought up..." '

This is a description of the kind of school Lowood is, and its role in making pupils aware of their 'humble position' as poor members of the middle class. The pupils' appearance emphasises their inferiority, and Mr Brocklehurst takes pleasure in telling Mrs Reed what his own daughter Augusta said about this after visiting the school.

' "I am not deceitful: if I were,..." '

Mrs Reed

Jane will not allow Mrs Reed to call her deceitful. Her sense of injustice makes her angry and resentful and, after Mr Brocklehurst has gone, it forces her to speak her mind. Mrs Reed's reaction is interesting – she talks to Jane as 'an opponent of adult age' and is clearly shaken. This perhaps explains Mrs Reed's deathbed summons in Chapter 21.

'I would fain exercise...'

Jane's feelings of vengefulness soon turn sour and she yearns for some more satisfying feeling to comfort her. Unable to gain her usual comfort from books or from the black, frosty weather outside, she welcomes Bessie affectionately. The warmth of Bessie's invitation to tea and their exchange of rather guarded affection for each other is underlined by the final sentence: 'Even for me life had its gleams of sunshine.'

Jane Eyre

Chapter 5

Jane arrives at Lowood School. She likes Miss Temple and makes friends with Helen Burns.

'The afternoon came on wet...'

You will know already that the weather in *Jane Eyre* is used to indicate the moods of the characters, especially of Jane. So what do the wind and rain suggest here? For other examples, look back to Chapter 3 and also at the section near the start of this chapter, beginning 'The moon was set...'.

Nature and character

Notice the irony with which Jane describes the grace that is said after the students have tried to eat the disgusting, burnt porridge. Food usually represents comfort and well-being, but here it tells you something about Lowood.

'I was still looking at them...'

The superintendent of the school, Miss Temple, is a kind woman and is concerned for Jane when she arrives. Notice her reaction to the burnt porridge a little further into this chapter.

Miss Temple

Jane strikes up a conversation with an unknown girl, gaining courage to do so from their common interest in books. The book which is mentioned – *Rasselas* by Dr Johnson – is a serious work that suggests that the best way to endure life is through patience and the acceptance of one's fate. The reading of this book tells you something about Helen's character, just as Jane's lack of enthusiasm for it tells you about hers.

Helen Burns

'The only marked event of the afternoon'

Notice how Jane reacts to someone whom she sees enduring punishment passively. She is convinced that she would react very differently, but you will notice that when her turn comes, she reacts after all in the same way. This is because she has come under Helen's influence and is led by her example.

Jane Eyre

18

Chapter 6

Jane's impetuous, untrained character contrasts with humble, patient Helen Burns.

'In the course of the day...'

The contrast between the character of the two girls is very marked. Jane would not have reacted to unfair treatment the way Helen does. You can tell this from Jane's remark: 'I wondered at her silence'.

Given Jane's freedom-loving character, it is not surprising that the play-hour is her favourite time of day. Notice that Jane wishes the weather more violent, to match her mood.

' "But that teacher, Miss Scatcherd, is so cruel to you?" '

Helen's attitude to punishment contradicts everything Jane believes in. Jane's views are based on her instinctive reaction to injustice; Helen's on careful thought about things. But Jane already seems to be under Helen's influence: 'I suspected that she might be right...'.

'I heard her with wonder:...'

Jane's views are very different from the Christian view of 'love thy neighbour'. Helen tells Jane that 'Heathens and savage tribes' believe what Jane seems to believe. Helen is a Christian, who accepts injustice with humility. She believes that the wrongs people suffer on earth are irrelevant when set against the eternal life of the spirit: '...injustice never crushes me too low: I live in calm, looking to the end.'

Chapter 7

Jane's first winter at Lowood is characterised by cold and hunger. Mr Brocklehurst is a cruel hypocrite and his visit culminates in Jane's public humiliation. Thanks to Helen's help, Jane is able to cope with this calmly.

' "Your directions shall be attended to, sir," said Miss Temple.'

Mr Brocklehurst's attitude tells you how unpleasant he is when he describes giving the girls a lunch of bread and cheese as encouraging 'habits of luxury and indulgence' and the inedible burnt porridge as a 'little accidental disappointment of the appetite'. His views are so extreme that you know he is insincere and Miss Temple's reaction underlines this.

'Meantime, Mr Brocklehurst, standing on the hearth...'

Mr Brocklehurst does not care whether Julia Severn's curly hair is natural or not. He wants the pupils to be children of God. Brontë here emphasises the contrast between the natural world and the world of strict religious views. Notice this contrast between Jane and Helen in Chapters 6 and 9.

Appearances

Education

You need to be clear on the various forms of cruelty practised at Lowood. Much of the suffering and humiliation derives from a debased Christian doctrine and awareness of the pupils' inferior social status: 'to render them hardy, patient, self-denying'.

' "All these top-knots must be cut off." '

Mr Brocklehurst's hypocrisy is emphasised when his wife and daughters arrive in the middle of his lecture about sobriety and vanity. Notice how little his own family worry about the need to 'mortify…the lusts of the flesh'. Mr Brocklehurst would not understand this irony. His views on the education of poor middle-class children were clearly set out in Chapter 4.

'The kind whisper went to my heart like a dagger.'

The public humiliation Mr Brocklehurst imposes on Jane is more evidence of his cruelty and the gap between what he says about Christian values and his own behaviour. Compare him with Miss Temple, who encourages the children 'by precept and example'.

'Mr Brocklehurst resumed.'

Mr Brocklehurst's description of Mrs Reed shows his lack of intelligence and sensitivity. In spite of his picture of himself as a great Christian, he punishes Jane harshly without any proof that she has done anything wrong.

'There was I, then, mounted aloft…'

In the past, when she has been unjustly treated, Jane has reacted strongly. Here she behaves very differently because she has been influenced by Helen's approach to life. Helen's look at Jane sustains her: like Miss Temple, Helen has a 'glow' in her eyes.

Chapter 8

Jane comes to terms with life at Lowood and prefers it to Gateshead. She learns to endure the poor conditions, thanks to the friendship of Helen and of Miss Temple, who helps her to clear her name. Jane is starting to see the value of Helen's patient, tolerant approach to life, but her passionate nature still erupts in the face of injustice.

'No; I know I should think…'

Jane is upset after her public humiliation because she fears that she will lose the love of those she cares about at Lowood. Helen warns that she thinks 'too

Love and passion

much of the love of human beings...' and encourages her to think beyond this life to God. Helen comforts her with the belief that God knows the truth about Jane. Although it seems unlikely that Jane shares Helen's view, the words give her comfort.

'Resting my head on Helen's shoulder...'

Miss Temple

Notice how Miss Temple's arrival coincides with the moon shining through the window. In Chapter 5 you saw how darkness meant despair and unhappiness, but here the moon's light signifies hope and warmth in the person of Miss Temple. Contrast the cheerfulness of Miss Temple's room with the rest of the school. Notice how fire is used as a symbol of comfort. The description of Miss Temple's room adds to what you already know about her character.

Education

Charlotte Brontë's attacks on education are not negative: she offers an ideal alternative as well. Miss Temple's qualities, like Helen's, are a mixture of the scholarly ('What stores of knowledge they possessed!') and the personal ('serenity ... kindness'). The combination inspires 'awe' and 'amazement'.

' "How are you tonight, Helen?" '

Helen Burns

There are several signs in this chapter that Helen is seriously ill. Notice the careful way Brontë is preparing you for Helen's death. You know from what Helen has said to Jane that she is prepared for her own death.

Jane's behaviour has already begun to change under Helen's influence. Her admiration of Helen increases, as she listens to their conversation. Helen clearly has a maturity far greater than her years.

'Next morning Miss Scatcherd wrote in conspicuous characters...'

Jane Eyre

Although Jane has seen Helen's example of humility, she still cannot remain unmoved in the face of injustice. Notice her anger at Helen's treatment and the strength of the bond between them.

'Thus relieved of a grievous load...'

Just as at Gateshead, Jane's life is made easier by the power of her dreams and her imagination. The final sentence in this chapter emphasises this.

Chapter 9

Spring arrives and there is an epidemic of typhus. This results in better food and conditions for those pupils who stay healthy. Helen falls ill and faces her death peacefully, certain of her life to come with God in heaven.

'April advanced to May...'

The first two pages of this chapter describe how Jane responds to the change in season. Contrasts are drawn between conditions inside and outside Lowood. Brontë makes use of this contrast for dramatic effect on many occasions, especially in Chapter 26. For the first time in her life, Jane has 'almost unlimited licence' to do as she wants. Jane has everything that gives her pleasure:

Environment   good weather, sufficient food, plentiful conversation.

'And where, in the meantime, was Helen Burns?'

Jane has strong feelings of affection and love for Helen. Notice how Jane's thoughts reveal the idea that love is returned for love.

Brontë introduces Jane's thoughts about Heaven and Hell at this particular moment for a good reason. Helen Burns is dying. Jane creeps up to Helen's sick-bed and the conversation

Nature and character   between the two girls shows how differently they feel about Helen's coming death.

Romance and mystery

Where this novel most differs from a typical romance is in the spiritual and religious element. Brontë may attack selfish and hypocritical Christians and criticise obsessive strictness, but the faith of Helen is presented as an ideal.

' "And shall I see you again, Helen, when I die?" '

Jane and Helen are very different in their personalities and their beliefs. You can see this in their differing attitudes to an afterlife. Helen's death is peaceful because, for her, Heaven is a certainty – hence her tombstone inscription 'Resurgam', which means 'I will arise'. Jane cannot think beyond the present, because her sensitivity to the natural world is still very great.

'Her grave is in Brocklebridge churchyard.'

Look at the last few lines of this chapter. Where did the marble tablet come from, do you think? This is skilful use of the 'narrator' technique by Brontë, who changes her time-perspective at different places in the story. Here you see a switch from the young Jane, telling you from the bedside of the dying Helen, to a much older Jane, telling you of her memories of that time. Usually, Brontë's use of the 'narrator' technique is obvious, but there are many other occasions – like here – where it is used with considerable subtlety.

Chapter 10

Lowood changes for the better after the typhus epidemic. Jane stays there for another eight years, the last two as a teacher. Miss Temple leaves and Jane, feeling restless, finds a new position as a governess.

'When the typhus fever had fulfilled...'

Brontë covers the next eight years of Jane's life swiftly. Changes are made after the typhus epidemic, and a management committee is formed to run Lowood. These men, who know how to run the school properly, draw attention to the things Mr Brocklehurst failed to do and they limit his influence.

'I went to my window, opened it, and looked out.'

Miss Temple was more than just a teacher to Jane. Through her friendship and example, Jane was not only re-educated, but her character was shaped as well. The influence of the natural landscape invites her to become adventurous again and reawakens her desire for liberty.

'Did She send you here, Bessie?'

Jane leaves Lowood. She is conscious of her own lack of physical beauty and still thinks that this will prevent her from ever being popular. This scene with Bessie tells you how far Jane has been educated as a 'lady'. Bessie says that Jane's accomplishments equal those of the Reed children. Notice what the accomplishments of a 'lady' were in those days: being 'genteel' (having good breeding), having a certain way of dressing, being able to play the piano and to draw, to speak French, and to sew decoratively. Interestingly, you learn here that Jane's relatives were not the poor folk Mrs Reed would have had her believe – Mr Eyre (brother to Jane's father) has visited Gateshead and to Bessie 'looked quite a gentleman'. This becomes important later – see Chapter 30.

Chapter 11

Jane takes a post as governess at Thornfield. She is relieved to learn that Mrs Fairfax is not the owner but the housekeeper. Jane meets her pupil, Adèle, who is a lively, extrovert child.

'Reader, though I look comfortably accommodated...'

Jane experiences a mixture of feelings when she thinks about her current situation. She runs through the positive and negative sides of being alone: freedom set against having no one to meet her; the excitement of adventure against the fear of loneliness.

She decides that even if Mrs Fairfax turns out to be no better than Mrs Reed, it does not matter: she can always re-advertise, because she no longer has to stay anywhere she does not want to.

Independence

' "Will you walk this way, ma'am," said the girl.'

Jane's welcome at Thornfield is warmer than she expected. Although Mrs Fairfax seems very much as Jane imagined, she is still surprised to be shown such kindness. Again, fire sets the background to Jane's sense of well-being.

Jane takes to Mrs Fairfax because they both are looking for the same thing – companionship. Jane has not been shown kindness very much before, and so she does not take it for granted – hence her gratitude towards Mrs Fairfax. Many references to other 'home comforts' appear in this chapter.

Jane Eyre

'When we left the dining room...'

The upper storeys of Thornfield are full of old, strangely carved and embroidered furniture and are surrounded by a strong atmosphere of mystery. There are references to possible supernatural activity, preparing you for strange events later.

The countryside around is agreeable but unexceptional. Brontë places this description here so that the normality of the surroundings contrasts to the shock of the mysterious laughter, which follows. The sight of ordinary-looking Grace Poole makes Jane even more certain that there is a straightforward explanation for it.

Supernatural and spiritual

Chapter 12

Jane begins to feel restless at Thornfield. She wishes to experience more of life. She meets Mr Rochester unexpectedly. The features of their final relationship are present at the start – they are instantly and instinctively drawn to each other and there is a spiritual aura of mystery surrounding their relationship.

'The promise of a smooth career...'

Adèle's character is summed up rather coolly. She is average in her abilities and easily taught. The bond between Adèle and Jane is not very close, though it is clear that she and Adèle like each other. Whilst Jane craves affection and love, her experience of life makes her wary of forming strong bonds of affection with people.

'Anybody may blame me who likes...'

The education of Adèle and the company of Mrs Fairfax are not fulfilling enough for Jane. Her instincts tell her that there are greater things to be had from life. Notice how you are being prepared for the arrival of Mr Rochester. When life is unstimulating, Jane resorts to her imagination as a means of escape (see Chapters 1 and 8). Here, her imagination creates stories of 'life, fire, feeling'. Fire is used here to symbolise passion and becomes real later when the frenzy of Bertha is unleashed and she burns down the house.

'It is in vain to say human beings ought to be satisfied...'

In this important passage, Brontë – through Jane Eyre – makes a plea for equality between men and women. In the nineteenth century, more women were becoming aware of the lack of opportunities for them. Often their only choice was to be a governess or paid companion.

Independence

'When thus alone, I not infrequently...'

Grace Poole is a woman of few words and unattractive appearance who, at times, likes a drink. You are left wondering whether she really seems the kind of person who would let out the terrible cries that Jane hears.

'The din was on the causeway...'

The first appearance of Mr Rochester is linked to supernatural images. This element is present throughout the courtship of Jane and Mr Rochester and gives his character an otherworldly, mysterious, slightly dangerous edge.

Supernatural and spiritual

Jane notices that Rochester is illuminated more by the light of the moon than the sun, which adds to the mystery of their meeting. She is conscious of his lack of beauty, but is already attracted to him.

Examiner's tip

In tackling the essay title on page 66, you should take note of the ways in which Rochester and Rivers are first introduced. This first appearance of Rochester also increases the sense of **Romance and mystery**: do we anticipate a bold lover, a cruel squire or both?

His 'frown and roughness' make her feel natural and at ease, whilst her concern for his well-being strikes him immediately.

The description of Rochester leaning on Jane is symbolic of their relationship. The words 'lean on me' recur in Chapters 19 and 26, symbolising the way they come to depend on one another.

'I did not like re-entering Thornfield.'

Notice that Jane feels her 'monotonous life' is now changed. Not only is she pleased to have made the acquaintance of a man, but she is attracted by one

so 'dark, strong and stern'. She does not look forward to returning to Thornfield, 'to stagnation', after the 'faint excitement' of her encounter.

The dog's name, Pilot, is emphasised. This is important, because he leads Rochester to Jane and gives the first clue to Jane about Rochester's identity.

Chapter 13

Thornfield seems a more cheerful place to Jane now that Mr Rochester is there. She finds his manner abrupt, but is not afraid of him and their conversation is lighthearted. Mrs Fairfax tells of the mystery surrounding his background, perhaps explaining his moodiness.

' "Is it necessary to change my frock?" '

Jane chooses the correct dress to suit the formality of the occasion. By choosing

the black dress and not the grey one, she signals that the meeting is not one at which she wants to look 'too fine'.

The description of Mr Rochester's face reveals a man who is striking but not handsome, seemingly grim and unsmiling. His lack of grace and polish sets Jane at her ease. She is intrigued by him.

Appearances

' "Eight years! You must be tenacious of life." '

Rochester comments that eight years at Lowood has left its mark on Jane, who is now eighteen years old. He remarks that she has 'the look of another world', and teases her, by suggesting that she may have bewitched his horse and that she was waiting for 'the men in green' when she sat on the stile in the moonlight. There is an instant rapport between them, as is shown by way in which Jane understands the teasing but Mrs Fairfax is puzzled by it.

Supernatural and spiritual

The mystery grows around Mr Rochester's character. His abruptness is explained partly by his nature, but Mrs Fairfax says he has family troubles, including the loss of his elder brother a few years previously. Jane suspects that Mrs Fairfax is being evasive and that Mr Rochester's behaviour also has to do with some strange, unknown event in the past which causes him to suffer.

Chapter 14

The relationship between Jane and Mr Rochester develops. The traditional master-servant relationship has been dispensed with and they are clearly attracted to each other.

' "Ah! By my word!" '

Mr Rochester is taken aback by Jane's frankness but, rather than take offence,

Appearances

he makes it an excuse to be frank himself. He mentions the 'prominences' on his head, which should show that he has a conscience – a reference to phrenology, or the study of the skull as a means of telling character, which was popular in the nineteenth century. He is stung when Jane asks him whether he is a philanthropist. In the nineteenth century it was an the mark of a gentleman to give thought to the poor and to be a philanthropist was therefore to be admired. Rochester admits that he has been hardened by life, but is hopeful of recovering sensitivity. It is Jane who will bring this change about.

' "You are dumb, Miss Eyre." '

Up to this point Rochester has had control of the situation, with Mrs Fairfax

Independence

and Adèle obedient to his orders. But Jane refuses to do as he wishes. At 38, Rochester is twenty years older than she is, but her 'Do as you please, sir' emphasises that she retains her right of independent thinking. She is not above teasing Mr Rochester about her role as 'paid subordinate', and her smile pleases him.

Examiner's tip

In writing of the character of Rochester and his relationship with Jane, it is necessary to be aware of the contrasts, even contradictions, which are perhaps necessary in a character who is admirable, yet sinful. His tolerance here contrasts with hints of a dark past and 'Gothic' horrors.

' "And so may you," I thought.'

Mr Rochester's experience is contrasted with Jane's unworldliness, and his cynicism with her idealism. He has already referred to her twice as 'nun-like' (Chapter 13). He envies the innocence her sheltered life has given her.

Rochester says that nature intended him to be a good man but events robbed him of his innocence: 'fate wronged me'. Again his mysterious past is hinted at.

' "Then you will degenerate still more, sir." '

Jane criticises Rochester's pursuit of pleasure. She recommends reform and repentance, but uses common sense and his own self-confession rather than self-righteousness. She is clearly concerned for him.

Rochester says 'You are not my conscience-keeper', but this is not true. Part of Jane's attraction for Rochester is based on his desire to lead a better life and to do what is right. He values her for her innocence, her unworldliness, her honesty and her consideration for him.

' "I am laying down good intentions..." '

This conversation (which Jane says is 'all darkness' to her) contains premonitions of future events: 'unheard-of combinations' and 'let it be right' echo in Mr Rochester's conscience later when he decides to go ahead with a bigamous marriage to Jane.

> **Bertha/Antoinette**
>
> Mrs Rochester's influence is much greater than her few brief appearances, not only in the mysteries of the third floor (with Jane at first completely misunderstanding the role of Grace Poole), but in these hints of a thorny moral problem.

Jane is still reserved and serious with Rochester, but he senses that as her confidence increases, her vivacity will emerge. He says she is like a caged bird; 'a vivid, restless, resolute captive' that will one day be free to soar into the sky.

Birds

Chapter 15

When Jane learns the truth about Adèle's origins and hears about Céline Varens, she finds a new sympathy for her. The mystery of Thornfield deepens as Rochester reveals his strange and deep dislike of the house. Late one night, Jane hears laughter and, when she investigates, she finds Rochester's bed is on fire. The incident brings them closer and makes them aware of the emotional bond between them.

'We were ascending the avenue...'

There is a marked Gothic element in this dramatic description of Mr Rochester as he looks up towards the battlements. Vivid language describes his facial expressions: 'wild', 'wrestle', 'pupil dilating', 'petrified his countenance'.

Mr Rochester compares destiny to a witch, but is determined to fly in the face of destiny nonetheless. This is another premonition of his later attempt to marry Jane. Already Rochester sees Jane as a possible source of happiness and, more importantly, a way of returning to 'goodness'.

Romance and mystery

The mystery of Rochester builds up around his desperate struggle with his destiny: 'a hag like one of those who appeared to Macbeth on the heath of Forres' - not a cheering comparison! There are other mysterious hags: Bertha and (as a kind of parody) 'the gypsy woman'.

' "No: Adèle is not answerable..." '

Jane's feelings towards Adèle grow warmer now that she knows the child is an orphan, but still finds her superficial (which she assumes is due to her 'Frenchness') and is troubled that the child is not more liked by Mr Rochester. Jane blossoms as she and Mr Rochester grow closer. He has become like 'a relation' now and she feels that they take mutual pleasure in the evenings that they spend together.

'And was Mr Rochester now ugly...'

People do not see ugliness where they find love: the person's personality shines

Appearances

through – but Jane does not yet fully realise that this also applies to her. Again the imagery of fire suggests comfort. Although she is not blind to Rochester's faults, Jane sees them as the result of 'circumstances', 'education' and 'destiny', and that there is great potential for good in him.

Dreams

The fire confirms Rochester's suspicions that Jane has been 'sent' to him. For the first time, Jane notices passion in his face: 'Strange energy was in his voice...'. At important points in the book Jane has vivid dreams. Here, she dreams she is tossed upon a wild sea but can see a beautiful shore that she is desperate to reach. The incident of the fire in Rochester's room makes them both aware that they may be falling in love, but neither speaks of it.

Examiner's tip

In preparing for an examination, there are certain key moments for especial revision. This one, placed pointedly at the end of Volume 1, is one such. It is, of course, of great importance for the Examination essay on page 66, plus the **Antoinette/ Bertha** and **Romance and mystery** coursework titles.

■ Self-test questions Chapters 1–15 (Volume 1)

Uncover the plot

Delete two of the three alternatives given, to find the correct plot. Beware possible misconceptions and muddles.

Jane lives with Mrs Reed/Mr Reed/Mrs Eyre at Brocklehurst/Lowood/Gateshead Hall: even the nurse Abbot/ Bessie/Eliza calls her 'less than a slave/lady/servant'. Fighting Georgiana/St John/John Reed, she is locked in the nursery/kitchen/redroom, and has a tantrum/fit/dream. A physician/apothecary/ clergyman suggests a school/convent/poorhouse. Mr Lloyd/Brocklehurst/Broughton accepts her for Gateshead/Millcote/Lowood school, where her first breakfast is oat cake/toast/ burnt porridge. She meets Helen Smith/Burns/Temple, who patiently/violently/ despairingly suffers the injustices of Miss Miller/Scatcherd/Pierrot, and sustains Jane when Mr Brocklehurst/Miss Scatcherd/Mrs Reed 'exposes' her as a liar/thief/ slattern. Jane also loves the superintendent Miss Smith/Miller/Temple. One spring/winter/summer, the school is hit by influenza/ consumption/typhus: Helen dies of influenza/consumption/typhus. Later, when Jane is a teacher/ superintendent/ pupil, Miss Temple dies/marries/retires, and Jane leaves to be a maid/governess/ nurse.

At Thornfield/Ferndean/Moor House, Jane is welcomed by Mrs Rochester/ Varens/Fairfax, the mistress/house-keeper/nurse, and her pupil Adèle/Blanche/Céline. On the second/third/attic floor, she hears a laugh/cry/crash: Grace Poole/Rochester/Bluebeard? One still/noisy/windy day, Jane meets Rochester/ Carter/Fairfax when his horse passes/bolts/falls. Conversations follow: about Bertha/Jane/Adèle and her paintings, and about Rochester – his hopes of forgiveness/reformation/marriage, and his betrayal by Celine/Adèle/Bertha. Jane saves Rochester from a fire/flood/attack.

Who? What? Why? How?

1 Who is Jane's father, and what do we learn about him and his family?
2 Whom does Jane remember positively at Gateshead and at Lowood?
3 What two punishments are inflicted on Jane in this section, and how does she react to them?
4 What three events at Lowood most impress themselves on Jane's memory, and the reader's mind?
5 What makes life tolerable for Jane at Lowood (a) despite the 'privations' and (b) when they end?
6 Why does Jane speak 'coolly' of Adele at first, and what changes her attitude?
7 Why does Jane decide to leave Lowood to become a governess?

8 How does Jane gain her 'first victory' over Mrs Reed, and what impels her to the 'battle'?
9 How do the smaller girls suffer at Lowood?
10 How does Mr Brocklehurst justify the poor food and facilities at Lowood?

Mirror images
Helen Burns offers a 'mirror' to other characters. What is the 'reverse image' of the following views of Helen's?
1 'It is far better to endure patiently a smart which nobody feels but yourself, than to commit a hasty action...' (6)
2 'Love your enemies; bless them that curse you.' (6)
3 'It (death) makes eternity a rest – a mighty home – not a terror and an abyss.' (6)
4 'The sovereign Hand... has provided you with other resources than your feeble self, or than creatures as feeble as you.' (8)
5 'God is my father; God is my friend; I love Him; I believe He loves me.' (9)

Looking forward to it?
Why might the following events strike you particularly, if you know what happens later in the novel?
1 Jane's attention is first called to Helen Burns by 'the sound of a cough'. (5)
2 Mrs Reed has told Jane that her Eyre relations are 'a beggarly set'. (3)
3 Jane vows: 'I will never call you aunt again... I will never come to see you when I am grown up'. (4)
4 Jane pictures Thornfield, from Mrs Fairfax's letter as 'a neat orderly spot'. (10)

Familiar themes
Many of the themes and images of Jane Eyre have been introduced in this section of the novel. Let's explore...
1 What images are associated with (a) Mr Brocklehurst and (b) Miss Temple?
2 What books has Jane read? What books are linked with (a) Bessie and (b) Helen?
3 What two meanings does the image of fire have – and why is it particularly significant later?
4 Give THREE examples of words in Chapter 2 associated with resistance and rebellion.
5 How is the appearance of (a) John, (b) Jane and (c) the Misses Brocklehurst used?

The odd couple
Let's explore the emerging relationship between Jane and Rochester.
1 What features of their first meeting are symbolic of the later relationship?
2 What superiority does Rochester claim over Jane?
3 When does Rochester literally lean on Jane, and how is this symbolic of their relationship?
4 What qualities does Rochester recognise and value in Jane?

Chapter 16

Jane is surprised when Rochester departs suddenly. When she finds out about Blanche Ingram, she decides that it is foolish for her to think that he could have any special feelings for her. She draws her own portrait in chalk and paints a picture of Blanche in oils to show how badly she compares with Blanche.

'I hastened to drive from my mind…'

Jane is aware of the change in her own appearance since she arrived at Thornfield. Much of this is due to Mr Rochester's presence. You may well wonder whether Mr Rochester's departure that morning was not partly due to a reluctance to have to face Jane's questions.

Appearances

' "Tall, fine bust, sloping shoulders; long graceful neck…" '

Mrs Fairfax's description of Miss Blanche Ingram brings Jane down to earth. She decides that she was foolish to imagine that Mr Rochester could have any special feeling for her, a plain governess. She makes herself draw her own portrait in chalk and Blanche Ingram's in oils and then compares the two. She is deliberately hard on herself in choosing the materials for the two pictures. The words she uses for her own portrait ('Portrait of a governess, disconnected, poor, and plain') are the opposite of what was considered desirable in young women seeking marriage.

Jane Eyre

Chapter 17

Mr Rochester returns with a party of guests, one of whom is Blanche Ingram. Grace Poole still intrigues Jane. Jane and Adèle are invited into the drawing-room on the following night and Jane is struck by the elaborate costumes and arrogant expressions of the guests. She finds Blanche beautiful but proud, and admits that she herself loves Mr Rochester. Jane attempts to leave the room, but Mr Rochester tells her he expects her to be present every evening while the guests are there.

'You have nothing to do with the master of Thornfield…'

Jane has a strong sense of her 'place' in the 'order' of society. She tells herself that it is undignified to show affection towards someone who is not for her. In spite of all this, her reaction to Rochester's letter shows she has not succeeded in gaining control of her feelings as she pretends.

Jane Eyre

'The strangest thing of all was…'

The mystery surrounding Grace deepens as Jane hears gossip concerning how highly she is paid for a difficult task. She is curious, and keen to find out the truth, but she is sure that she is being deliberately kept in the dark.

Jane is critical of Adèle's love of dressing up in fine clothes. Jane's preference for plain clothes (seen in Chapters 11 and 13) is her way of saying that she is hiding nothing. In contrast to Jane's simple clothes, notice the rich, fine clothes of Rochester's guests. They look like 'a flock of white, plumy birds'.

Appearances

'As far as person went, she answered point for point…'

Remember, as you read this, that Jane is describing Blanche Ingram and that she may be biased. Jane admits that Blanche is a great beauty, but stresses that she seems haughty and self-conscious.

'Most true it is that "beauty is in the eye of the gazer".'

This is the first time that Jane admits to herself that she loves Mr Rochester. Look back at their conversations in Chapters 13 and 14 to see how far you can confirm Jane's view that Rochester and herself have 'certain tastes and feelings in common'. Jane admits here that to deny her love for Mr Rochester would be to deny her natural feelings.

Love and passion

'I feared – or should I say hoped?'

Blanche's unpleasant character is revealed by the spiteful way she talks about her treatment of her own governesses, dismissing them as 'nuisances'. Note the care with which Rochester speaks to the female guests, purposely avoiding saying anything hurtful to Jane, leading them into revealing their true natures for him and Jane to observe.

Social class

' "How do you do?" he asked.'

Rochester senses Jane's unhappiness and this brief meeting in the hall shows that he is not really the sort of person he has been pretending to be with his guests. You can imagine what he might have been about to say before he stopped himself, when he said 'Goodnight, my…?'

Love and passion

Chapter 18

The party of guests play charades. Jane decides that if Mr Rochester marries Blanche it will not be for love. While Rochester is absent one day on business, the guests are surprised by the arrival of a stranger from the West Indies. An intriguing situation is created at the end of the chapter by the arrival of a gypsy, who wants to tell the fortunes of all the female guests.

' "Will you play?" he asked.'

Appearances

The charades emphasise the play-acting that seems typical of the lives of the guests. Notice the irony of Blanche and Rochester acting out a marriage associated with imprisonment: Bridewell was a prison in London. Rochester plays the part of a prisoner there – he is in many ways a prisoner of his circumstances, just as mad Bertha is a prisoner upstairs.

'I saw he was going to marry her…'

Jane senses that Rochester does not love Blanche. She therefore concludes that he is going to marry her for reasons that were customary then amongst people of his class – she will secure him 'rank and connections' in society.

Social class

Jane senses that Blanche is play-acting to win Mr Rochester's affection. Ironically, Jane feels she could teach her a few lessons on how to win his heart. Jane has a very idealistic view of love and does not understand the idea of a 'marriage of convenience', which was so common among upper-class people at that time.

'The want of his animating influence appeared to be…'

In Mr Rochester's absence, everything becomes dreary. Again the weather outside matches the mood in the writing, and you see books used to raise spirits.

'His manner was polite; his accent, in speaking, struck me…'

You get an unfavourable impression of Mr Mason. His face is attractive but it lacks force and intelligence. Inevitably, Jane compares him with Mr Rochester and she is struck by the contrast between them. As if to emphasise the immense gulf between Jane and the other ladies, Brontë shows how they form quite different impressions of Mr Mason.

Chapter 19

Jane meets the gypsy fortune-teller, but carefully avoids telling her anything about her feelings for Mr Rochester. Jane seems unsurprised when the gypsy turns out to be Mr Rochester in disguise, but is annoyed by the deception. Mr Rochester seems deeply shocked by the arrival of Mr Mason.

' "Your fortune is yet doubtful: when I examined your face…" '

Jane's plain speaking and directness is noticeable during the episode with 'the gypsy'. Rochester knows that she is a clever opponent who will not betray his confidence. What he says here could easily be Jane talking to herself after

Independence

finding out about Bertha. Rochester recognises Jane's independence and deep-rooted integrity, and is convinced that he must keep Bertha's identity a secret. From this passage it is clear that Rochester has already decided to ask Jane to marry him. When Rochester brings his ramblings to a sudden halt, it is clear that Jane is not the only one who has to keep emotions in check.

' "Well, Jane, do you know me?" '

Jane Eyre

Jane's reaction to discovering the identity of the gypsy is a mixture of surprise and irritation. She does not admit to being deceived, although she believed it was Grace Poole and never suspected it might be Rochester. She is pleased to be told that she has been careful what she said because much of it was about her feelings for Rochester, which she wants to keep to herself.

' "The devil he did!" '

Rochester's reaction to the sudden arrival of Mr Mason is puzzling. This is another mystery here, and mention of the West Indies adds to it.

' "To comfort me?" '

Love and passion

Jane says she is willing to put up with the disapproval of other people for Rochester's sake. About a page before, Jane again invited Rochester to 'lean on me' – a symbol of their increasing dependence on one other. To protect her feelings, Jane hurriedly adds that she would do just as much for any friend.

Chapter 20

Bloodcurdling cries awaken the household. Rochester assures the guests that all is well, and then asks Jane to come up to the attic. She finds Mr Mason badly wounded and tends his injuries until Mr Rochester returns with a doctor. Mr Mason is smuggled away before daybreak. Mr Rochester tells Jane about his past life and is about to say he loves her, but then changes the subject to his proposed marriage to Blanche Ingram.

' "Good god! What a cry!" '

Supernatural and spiritual

Notice the language that is used to describe this terrifying cry and the fear that Jane feels on hearing it: 'savage', 'sharp', 'paralysed'. The timing of the scream, just after a description of the moonlight, adds to the Gothic atmosphere.

The mystery increases when Jane is taken up to the attic and hears it again. It is unlike anything human, 'almost like a dog quarrelling'. Jane naturally assumes that it is Grace Poole. The suspense is prolonged, as both Jane and Mr Mason are forbidden to speak to each other.

The language which describes Mr Mason's wounds is also part of the Gothic tradition of writing: 'wild beast' and 'fiend'.

Examiner's tip

Another key chapter for examination revision, this is notable for the de-humanisation of Bertha. Is she an evil spirit ('goblin', 'a mocking demon'), a wild animal ('snarling', 'a dog quarrelling') or a mighty bird ('the widest-winged condor on the Andes', 'a carrion-seeking bird of prey')? This is also important for the coursework title on **Bertha/Antoinette**.

'And this man I bent over – this commonplace, quiet stranger...'

The impact of Mr Mason's arrival on Rochester is compared to the impact of a thunderbolt on an oak tree. Compare a similar image at the end of Chapter 23. On both occasions the symbolism is of something natural and strong that has struggled to grow over many years, only to be split apart by lightning in a moment. The tree represents the strength of Rochester's character – or their love for each other – and the lightning conveys the destructive power of fate over their lives.

' "It seems to me a splendid mansion, sir." '

There is a vivid contrast between the language used to describe the garden and that used to describe the house. The flowers are 'fresh' and 'fragrant' but the house is described with horror. Rochester feels this way about the house now because Bertha – who represents his dark past – lives there. He prefers the garden because Jane is there and she symbolises his hopes for a brighter future.

Environment

' "Well, then, Jane, call to aid your fancy..." '

Rochester conveys a powerful, natural spirituality and moral sense here: he believes strongly in the possibility of redemption. He tries to overcome his misgivings and win Jane's acceptance by justifying his future plans. He says he has committed an 'error' not a 'crime' and his marriage was a matter of 'custom' rather than morality. But clearly this is a real moral dilemma for him.

Mr Rochester

Perhaps rather surprisingly – given what you know already about her – Jane tells him to look to God for help. Rochester does not answer in full, because he thinks, perhaps, that he has found God's instrument for salvation in Jane.

Chapter 21

Jane is summoned to Gateshead, where her aunt is dying. Eliza and Georgiana are still unfriendly. Mrs Reed is also cold towards her and seems to have called for her out of a sense of guilt. She confesses that she lied to Jane's uncle, who wanted Jane to inherit his fortune. Jane forgives her aunt for the injustices she has done to her.

'Presentiments are strange things!'

Supernatural and spiritual

This first paragraph could easily be an explanation of where the voices come from, which send Jane back in search of Rochester at the end of Chapter 35. Notice how the practical side of Jane's mind tries to find some commonsense explanation for things which cannot be explained. Brontë suggests that dreams are a way of seeing into the future, and this is a typically Gothic theme which runs through the novel.

'At all events you *will* come back…'

Jane demonstrates her independence by taking only the amount of money that is owed to her. She does not want more, in spite of Mr Rochester's attempts to persuade her to take it.

'In such conversation an hour was soon gone…'

Independence

Jane feels able to face coming back to Gateshead because of her greater maturity and self-confidence. Two important factors which have helped to heal the wounds and free her from resentment are her greater independence and the fact that she no longer needs emotional support from the Reeds.

'Two young ladies appeared before me; one very tall…'

Jane's description shows Eliza in a very severe light. Her clothes are plain and her face is unattractive. The words 'sallow', 'colourless' and 'ascetic' describe the absence of any spark of humanity in her appearance.

Georgiana is quite a contrast to her sister, but is equally unappealing. Notice the words Jane uses to describe her: 'full-blown', 'languishing', 'blooming and luxuriant'. But she also says that Georgiana's face has an 'an indescribable hardness'. Eliza virtually ignores Jane, whilst Georgiana is critical and condescending towards her.

' "Mama dislikes being disturbed in an evening…" '

Jane Eyre

You see a more mature and wiser Jane here, able to put up with the indifference of her cousins, when previously she would have been sensitive to their unfriendliness. She is learning to allow her reason to rule her emotions. Later on, Jane will need all her powers of self-discipline to escape being trapped and separated forever from Rochester.

'Well did I remember Mrs Reed's face...'

The power of love is shown again here. Jane's happiness which comes from loving Rochester makes her more charitable. She can forgive and even feel sorry for her aunt.

Mrs Reed has not changed her opinion of Jane. To do so would mean admitting that she has treated her badly. We learn why she hated Jane from the start – her husband was always fond of his sister, Jane's mother, and defended her when the rest of the family wanted to disown her. When Jane's mother died, Mr Reed adopted and raised Jane as his own child, seeming to prefer her to his own children. Mrs Reed's dislike of Jane was based on jealousy, and that is why Jane feels sorry for her.

'Eliza still spoke little: she had evidently no time to talk.'

Eliza's life is busy but meaningless. She feels safe and happy only when doing something planned and organised. She has established her independence of other people, with 'safe barriers between herself and a frivolous world'. Notice that she has the same mercenary streak that she always had. The Reed girls lack any feeling for their mother – neither can wait until she is dead.

' "Georgiana, a more vain and absurd animal than you..." '

Eliza criticises her sister for preferring company and a life of pleasure. She says

a daily routine like her own would make Georgiana more independent. Her idea of independence is different from Jane's, because it is not natural, and excludes human affection.

The balance between nature and principle – or 'feeling and judgement' – is one of the major themes of the novel. Jane

Independence

compares feeling to a food that is too difficult to digest without the help of judgement.

'Poor, suffering woman!'

Although guilty conscience drove Mrs Reed to send for Jane, she is unable to accept her own guilt and the forgiveness which Jane readily offers. When her aunt dies, notice how Jane feels sadness for Mrs Reed's sufferings.

Chapter 22

On her way home, Jane steels herself to face the coming marriage of Mr Rochester and Blanche Ingram. She walks over the fields to Thornfield and meets Mr Rochester on the way. She is overwhelmed by her feelings of love for him and he seems to sense this. Everyone welcomes her back, and she settles into her old routine, hoping that somehow they will all be together after Rochester and Blanche are married. Strangely though, there is no more talk of weddings and Rochester makes no further visits to Blanche.

'It was not a bright or splendid summer...'

Again you see nature matching the mood of the scene. The hay is being gathered in and the roses are out in the hedgerows. The symbolism of this is ripeness and expectation – and the inevitability of a coming winter.

Nature and character

Jane experiences an inner struggle to keep control of her emotions when she sees Rochester. Brontë uses the image of a veil to convey Jane's efforts at self-control.

Look at the language Rochester uses and the way he describes Jane. His

view of her as 'other-worldly' underlines the idea that fate – or some other supernatural power – had meant them for each other all along.

Jane uses the imagery of a bird to describe herself. Here the bird is not caged but wild and free, grateful for the few bits of food (or comfort) that Rochester has to offer.

Birds

' "Thank you, Mr Rochester, for your great kindness." '

This is an important moment in the book. Jane, for once, allows her feelings to show when she speaks these words. This allows her to realise her ideal for the first time in her life – look at the sentence beginning: 'This was very pleasant...' She is welcomed and feels loved by all at Thornfield.

Love and passion

Chapter 23

Rochester tests Jane with his plans to send her to Ireland, but she breaks down at this 'news' and tells him of her love for him. He confesses his true feelings for her. The moment of perfection is broken by a storm, during which a lightning bolt strikes the chestnut tree and splits it in two – a symbol of the stroke of fate which will separate them.

'A splendid Midsummer shone...'

In this detailed description of her surroundings, notice how 'Eden-like' everything is for Jane: the weather, the countryside in its fullness, the hay gathered in, the trees 'full leaved', the sunset beautiful. Brontë emphasises Jane's extreme happiness, so that the contrast with what follows will seem even stronger.

Environment

'I walked a while on the pavement...'

There is an air of expectancy and the smell of cigar-smoke adds to this because it prepares us for Rochester's appearance.

Jane attempts to avoid Rochester in order not to disturb the idyllic mood. Notice the rapport that exists between them – even though she tries to move in silence, he knows she is there.

' "Very soon, my – that is, Miss Eyre..." '

Birds

Love and
passion

Rochester announces his marriage to Blanche and tells Jane she must leave because Adèle must go off to school. Notice how it is the song of a nightingale that finally frees Jane's feelings.

Jane summarises what she has loved about Thornfield and places special emphasis on her experiences of independence, intellectual life and love. This passage is Jane's passionate declaration of love.

Notice how this passage looks forward to the end of the book, when both have 'passed through the grave'.

Examiner's tip

There are many problems to understanding Rochester and his behaviour to Jane. Deceiving her over marriage to Blanche Ingram (which reaches its peak just before truth breaks out) can be seen as a test or a way of releasing Jane's feelings, but is it an honourable course of action?

' "Dear Edward!" '

Rochester still has a fearful secret. He worries about people 'meddling' and says defiantly that he doesn't care what other people think. Rochester says that he is making amends for his past misdeeds by marrying Jane. He is confident that God will forgive him everything.

The approaching storm and the fate of the chestnut tree symbolise the coming upheavals and future rift in their relationship.

Chapter 24

Jane shuns fine clothes and defends her right to choose. She makes clear her disapproval of the way Rochester has treated Blanche. She is upset by Mrs Fairfax's cool reaction to the news of her forthcoming marriage to Rochester. Jane keeps a distance between herself and Rochester, partly to ensure her own independence and partly because she is nervous about the strong feelings they have for each other.

'While arranging my hair...'

Notice the use of the image in the mirror again. Just as in the red-room, the

Appearances

mirror shows Jane's perception of herself, rather that the reality.

Love gives Jane new confidence and she feels that she is blossoming with happiness. There is a very clear connection here between Jane's surroundings and her mood: 'Nature must be gladsome when I was so happy.'

Independence

Just as she dislikes elaborate clothes, Jane rejects as 'unnatural' adornments like jewellery. She says she does not want to be an 'ape in a harlequin's jacket'.

Rochester talks about being 'healed and cleansed' by Jane. This repeats his view of her as an angel sent by God (see Chapters 13 and 14). Jane makes it quite clear that she will not conform to any of these images that he has of her: 'I will be myself'.

'The hour spent at Millcote...'

Despite her love for Rochester, Jane cannot bear to have expensive gifts

Independence

lavished on her. Her pride cannot endure the feeling of dependence that this brings.

Jane wants to hold on to her independent position as governess, to be self-sufficient and to earn her wages. She wants nothing more from Mr Rochester than to be allowed to love him and to be loved herself.

'He rose and came towards me...'

Jane is calculating in her behaviour towards Mr Rochester. She makes it very

Jane Eyre

clear that she is independent of him; she is not like an Indian wife who would commit 'suttee' (i.e. kill herself on her husband's funeral pyre). Her honesty is so strong that she is determined to show him all the sides of her character, pleasant and unpleasant, before he marries her.

She keeps Mr Rochester at arm's length by being deliberately difficult and provocative. She is aware of her passion for him and is reluctant to be dominated by him.

'Yet after all my task was not...'

Love and passion

Jane acknowledges the full intensity of her love for Rochester – to the point of idolatry. This is an important point to remember when you consider her reaction after she has found out about his wife.

Chapter 25

A month later, Jane tells Rochester about her dreams and a figure she has seen in her room. He says the figure was Grace Poole and Jane goes to bed feeling reassured.

'It was not without a certain wild pleasure...'

Environment

The driving wind echoes the agitation in Jane's mind, and the tree symbolises the rift between Jane and Rochester when the secret of his wife is revealed. The uneasy atmosphere, created by the 'blood red' moon which throws a 'dreary glance' and the 'wild, melancholy wail' of the wind, foreshadows the coming tragedy.

' "I dreamt another dream, sir..." '

Jane's dream about a child is another example of the way children symbolise

Dreams

hope and helplessness in the novel. Bessie has already said that dreams about children are a warning of trouble and this dream foreshadows events nearer the end of the novel. It reminds us of the spiritual side of Jane's nature.

As Jane's account of her dream reaches its climax, Gothic language describes the apparition – which is, of course, Bertha – 'fearful, ghostly, savage', 'bloodshot eyes'. The first time Jane became 'insensible from terror' was when she was imprisoned in the red-room, and this scene echoes the earlier one.

Chapter 26

Mr Rochester hurries Jane to the church. She sees two shadowy figures in the churchyard who are later responsible for stopping the marriage taking place. The truth about Mr Rochester's wife is revealed. Jane is taken to the attic room to visit Bertha, who behaves more like a wild animal than a human being. At first, Jane is numbed, but then feels a great sense of betrayal. She is overwhelmed by despair.

'At the churchyard wicket he stopped...'

Notice Rochester's haste to get to the church. He wants to get the marriage over with, before fate can intervene and ruin everything.

Bertha/Antoinette

Again the narrative reaches a climax at the end of a volume. The presentation of Bertha as a wild animal prevents the reader from regarding her as a human being with feelings: only Jane and Rochester's happiness matters. Jean Rhys' version restores her to beauty and humanity.

' "That is *my wife*, said he." '

Brontë uses exaggerated, Gothic language to describe Bertha's appearance: 'is

this beast or human?', 'grovelled', 'growled', 'grizzled hair', 'wild as a mare', 'clothed hyena', 'shaggy locks'.

Listen to Rochester's bitter and sarcastic tones when he says 'Such is the sole conjugal embrace I am ever to know'. His feelings about his plight are full of self-pity and self-justification.

'Jane Eyre, who had been an ardent, expectant woman…'

Jane makes the decision to leave. She does so not because it would be wrong to stay with Mr Rochester, but because she feels that he cannot possibly have been sincere in his feelings for her and cannot truly have loved her. She assumes that she will seem hateful to him now. Notice how her feelings are described through the weather and its effect on the landscape. This is one of the most beautiful and poignant descriptions in the book.

Environment

In her moment of desolation Jane turns towards God. Her 'remembrance of God' echoes the end of Chapter 24, where Jane says that Rochester has become so important in her life that he even displaces religion and stands between her and God.

■ Self-test questions Chapters 16–26 (Volume 2)

Uncover the plot

Delete two of the three alternatives given, to find the correct plot. Beware possible misconceptions and muddles.

After an absence of two days/a week/more than a fortnight, Rochester returns, bringing home a party, including Amy/Diana/Blanche Ingram. Jane now loves/hates/is indifferent to Rochester, while believing he will marry her/Blanche/Celine. Rochester, disguised as a witch/gypsy/servant, shows no/strong/negative feelings for Jane. After Rivers/Mason/Eshton is attacked, they walk in the house/field/garden. Rochester says only 'an obstacle of custom/convention/feeling' keeps him from a new life – but his 'cure' is Blanche/Jane/Adèle.

Jane visits a dying Mrs/John/Eliza Reed: only the house/Bessie/Jane has changed. Returning, Jane meets Rochester/Adèle/Bertha in the lane. One morning/evening/afternoon, he talks of a post in Ireland/London/ Scotland – but then renounces Blanche/Jane/Bertha, and proposes. Jane has visions/nightmares/hallucinations, and is terrified by Mason/Briggs/a madwoman. The wedding is stopped by Briggs/Grey/Green, with Mason/Fairfax/Poole as witness. Rochester confesses: his wife/mistress/sister Bertha is sane/alive/dead.

Who? What? Why? How?

1 Who, of the party guests, is the character most 'sympathetic' to Jane, and why?
2 Who reminds Jane of Mrs Reed?
3 What does the gypsy woman tell Jane that hints at Rochester's feelings for her?
4 What features of Blanche's appearance particularly contrast with Jane's?
5 What two letters alter events to prevent Jane's marriage to Rochester?
6 Why does the recognition of Blanche's inferiority hurt Jane even more?
7 Why did Mrs Reed dislike the child Jane, and why can she not forgive her to the end?
8 Why does Jane say she must leave Rochester, in Chapters 21, 23 and 26?
9 How do we know, on Mason's first appearance (Chapters 19-20) that he is somehow significant to, or involved in, the story?
10 How does Rochester 'test' Jane's feelings before his proposal to her?

Mirror images

1 Is Jane 'fair' in her comparison between her self-portrait and her picture of the imagined Blanche?
2 Compare Jane's and Blanche's view of what is important for a woman.
3 What qualities in Blanche's heart and mind make her the 'inferior' – and opposite – of Jane?
4 What does Mason have – and lack – that makes him the opposite of Rochester?

Make the connection

These key chapters are full of connections – between people, and between past and present. Let's explore...

1 What connects (a) Mason to Bertha? (b) Rochester to Bertha? (c) Mason to Rochester (before marriage)?
2 What connects (a) Mason to John Eyre? (b) Jane to John Eyre?
3 Give THREE examples of prior hints or 'premonitions' of the revelations at the wedding.
4 Give THREE examples of ideas or events which look forward to what happens at the end of the book.

Picture this!

Brontë uses imagery and symbolism in order to highlight themes in the novel. Let's explore...

1 Give TWO examples of how images of trees or plants are used to describe people.
2 Give examples of the positive and negative associations of (a) dogs and (b) birds. What do you notice?
3 To what effect are moonlight and sunlight used on the night when Mason is attacked? Compare this to the first meeting of Jane and Rochester (Chapter 12).

Family fortunes

1 What is the same, and what has changed, when Jane returns to her 'first' family at Gateshead?
2 What opportunity for family has Jane missed out on - and why does this become significant?
3 What suggests that Jane has 'adopted' a new family at Thornfield, which she then loses?
4 How does Jane (Chapter 21) confront the 'spectres' of her past. How does this compare to Rochester in the next volume (Chapter 27)?

Chapter 27

Jane realises that she must leave Thornfield. Rochester thinks that telling Jane the truth will persuade her to stay, but he is mistaken. Jane has a dream in which a voice urges her to leave and she sets off, unseen, early the next day.

'Some time in the afternoon...'

Independence

Jane struggles with her conscience, which tells her that she cannot rely on the help of others. Her words: 'you shall, yourself, pluck out your right eye...' are both a quotation from Matthew's Gospel and an allusion to Mr Rochester's fate.

Her sense of isolation – which she has not felt for a long time – returns in full: 'Friends always forget...'

'Reader! – I forgave him at the moment...'

Love and passion

Jane's initial reason for leaving – her doubts about his love for her – vanishes as soon as she sees Rochester – although she still feels that she must leave him, it will be much harder now that she is sure of his love.

Mr Rochester is not surprised by Jane's behaviour, because her reaction is just what he was expecting. However, unlike Jane, it has not occurred to him that she might leave.

' "Well, Jane, being so..." '

Mr Rochester admits that he was deceived by appearances. He thought that

Appearances

he loved his wife and, encouraged by their two families who thought it a 'good match', he married her. Make up your own mind about how far you think he was really deceived and how far this excuses his subsequent behaviour.

Mr Rochester discovered that he disliked his wife's behaviour – 'intemperate and unchaste' – long before she was declared insane. Again, decide yourself whether this gave him the right to disown her.

' "Go," said Hope, "and live again..." '

Social class

Rochester has convinced himself of the justice of his case. In his eyes he has no wife, and so feels free to look for someone else to love.

His account of his life during his ten years' wandering makes Rochester sound very much a man of the world. He admits that he kept a mistress, but is eager to point out that he never indulged in debauchery (depraved self-indulgence).

' "Why are you silent, Jane?" '

Jane's inner struggle is between two forces – one, the claims of her inner feelings and the other, her 'intolerable duty'. She is rebelling against her nature by doing what she believes to be right.

Nature and character

Rochester uses moral blackmail in order to keep Jane from leaving and, given the way he feels about her, you may be able to sympathise with him. He tries to arouse her pity by his question: 'Then you condemn me to live wretched...'

'Still indomitable was the reply...'

Jane is almost won over by Rochester's strongest argument – she has no family,

so who would she be offending? But look at the integrity in her answer: 'I care for myself.' She has to do what she feels is right. Rochester sees Jane's determined spirit shining through her eyes and knows that, even if he could somehow force her to stay, he would find himself with only 'the brittle frame' of her.

Jane Eyre

'That night I never thought to sleep...'

Jane again dreams about the red-room. The reason for this is that she is

experiencing the same feelings of isolation and rejection now as she did then. Notice that the same inner voice speaks to her here as at the start of the chapter – read the beginning and end of the chapter again to get a clearer idea of the role that is played by Jane's conscience during times of crisis.

Dreams

Jane likens her life to a book, but unlike those books which have previously consoled her in times of trouble, this one contains only a blank page where her future should be.

She also uses the bird image: 'birds were emblems of love'. The sound of birdsong hurts her because she is reminded of her deep sense of betrayal.

Chapter 28

Jane is put down by the coachman in open countryside and feels completely isolated. She is reduced to begging, but after two days she is taken in by the Rivers family.

'Whitcross is no town…'

Jane is set down in an isolated place where no houses or people are to be seen.

Her surroundings reflect her present circumstances – 'I have no relative…'. She compares her longing for Rochester to the feelings of a bird which yearns to fly but is powerless to do so.

Jane's rapport with nature is now restricted – she cannot survive on the fruits of nature alone, and is reduced to begging. This time, food is a symbol of Jane's destitution. Not even the pig wants the porridge, yet she 'devoured it ravenously'. The last time Jane was faced with ruined porridge, she couldn't eat it.

Environment

'Entering the gate and passing…'

The Rivers' house corresponds to Jane's ideal of safety and comfort: the fire, the books, the women's refined faces. Notice how strong a contrast it forms to Jane's previous desolation and discomfort. She feels she is no longer 'outcast' and is able to be herself again.

Romance and mystery

The arrival at St. John Rivers' house is as dramatic in its way as the arrival at Mr Rochester's. Starving and lost, Jane follows a light over hill and bog till she comes to a scene of serene domesticity framed in a window. It is a journey out of a fairy-tale.

Chapter 29

It takes Jane four days to recover from her state of exhaustion and starvation. She is well received by Diana and Mary Rivers, but the servant Hannah is resentful of her at first. Hannah tells Jane about the Rivers' family background. St John seems cold, insensitive and reserved. Jane admits to giving the family a false name but refuses to reveal her true one. St John agrees to try to find her work.

'On a chair by the bedside…'

Jane is always conscious of the impression of her physical appearance on others and is pleased that she is able to look respectable again.

Her pride has been wounded by her being reduced to begging.

Note again the two symbols of comfort – fire and food – that are used to express Jane's sense of peace and contentment at Moor House.

Appearances

'Mr St John – sitting as still as one of the dusky pictures…'

This description of St John shows you a character who is exactly the opposite of Mr Rochester. Jane cannot 'read' his eyes as she could Mr Rochester's. St John's eyes reveal nothing of his thoughts – they are only 'instruments to search with'. He questions Jane with curiosity about her circumstances, but is less understanding than his sisters. Notice her use of the words 'cold and stern' to describe him. You will find lots of images that are used by Brontë to reflect St John's coldness.

' "Indeed, you *shall* stay here…;" '

Diana and Mary are very pleasant, with Diana seeming the more open. They are welcoming and considerate, willing to offer Jane a home and to respect her privacy. Notice the recurrence of a familiar image in the novel, when they say that they want to look after Jane as they would 'a half-frozen bird'.

Chapter 30

Living with the Rivers girls at Moor House is a pleasant experience for Jane as they seem to have a lot in common. Diana and Mary get ready to return to their posts as governesses and St John asks Jane to take on the position of village schoolmistress. Despite its low status, Jane accepts the job because it gives her shelter and independence. The Rivers learn of the death of their uncle, which is a more significant event than any of them yet realise.

'I liked to read what they liked…'

This is a picture of complete harmony between Jane and the Rivers girls. They have a mutual love of books and they share their different talents, with Jane being taught German, while she teaches them about drawing.

Books

'No weather seemed to hinder him…'

St John is a diligent parson who lets nothing stand in the way of his duty. Jane

feels that he seems to lack the kind of contentment which should go with such a selfless life. She quickly realises that he is very different from his two sisters. He does not share their love of nature or their satisfaction in walking on the moors. Jane senses that beneath the eloquent sermoniser lies a dissatisfied man who, like her, is searching for fulfilment and peace of mind.

' "Do explain", I urged...'

St John's explanation gives an insight into how education was organised for

Social class

the poor in the early nineteenth century. They had to rely on the benevolence of the richer members of the community. Jane does not think the position of village schoolmistress very prestigious, but it will afford her two essential things: shelter and independence. In St John's own view, Jane's talents will be wasted in such 'monotonous labour wholly void of stimulus'.

'I was going to say, impassioned...'

Nature and character

St John speaks of his restlessness and reveals an awareness of the irony of his own position. He, who preaches to others about being content, cannot be so himself. He sees the gulf that exists between 'propensities and principles' – in other words, between his 'inclinations and beliefs'.

'Diana and Mary Rivers became more sad and silent...'

Diana recognises that St John will crush all his natural feelings in order to achieve his ambitions. She says 'He will sacrifice all' and thinks his decision is 'right' and 'noble', though she is sad at the thought of his leaving. Jane frequently uses images of stone and marble to describe St John's lack of emotions.

Examiner's tip

In writing on any main character in *Jane Eyre*, you need to note images that reflect Brontë's view of him/her. In this chapter St. John Rivers is characterised by metaphor ('the ice of reserve', 'marble immobility of feature') and simile ('inexorable as death').

Chapter 31

At first, Jane is not very enthusiastic about her job as schoolmistress, but is grateful for a home, and hopes that the improvement in her pupils will bring her satisfaction. She is not sure that she did the right thing by leaving Thornfield. St John is sure that he should obey God's will, but he pays a high price in his relationship with Miss Oliver.

'Was I very gleeful, settled...'

Jane Eyre

Jane is doing this job entirely out of a sense of duty and as a mark of her independence. She does not expect to get much in the way of personal enjoyment from it. She feels degraded because she has gone down in the world, but she has the sense to realise that getting to know the children might improve her liking for the job.

'Meantime, let me ask myself…'

This important passage sums up the major theme of this part of the book. The question is whether Jane was right to follow the moral code which her conscience told her she should, or whether she should have followed the inclinations of her own heart. The same dilemma confronts St John, and this idea is developed later. St John's sisters suggested in the last chapter that he is already going against his natural feelings by doing what he thinks is God's will. Here, Jane breaks out in tears because inside she knows she is denying her instincts. She has lost the close harmony between her surroundings and her nature.

Nature and character

' "Very well; I hope you feel…" '

Notice how unsympathetic St John is when he sees that Jane has been crying. He is 'grave almost to displeasure' and looks at her 'with austerity'. Rochester would never have reacted in this way. St John preaches at Jane, warning against dwelling too much on the past. He tells her that to control nature and follow principle 'is hard work'.

To illustrate this, St John relates his own experience. He says he was an ambitious man who was frustrated by the humble life of a parson. He suffered for a whole year before he finally understood that God wanted him to become a missionary. As you get to know St John's character better, you may be able to put another interpretation on his decision to become a missionary.

' "Good evening, Mr Rivers" '

Notice St John's reaction to Miss Oliver. First he will not look at her and, when he does, simply gazes at her without smiling. Jane understands instinctively that he is excited by Miss Oliver but that he holds himself tightly under control.

Only Jane can appreciate the effort of willpower it must have taken for St John to refuse Miss Oliver's invitation. Jane admits that he is as unyielding as Diana said he was. Decide for yourself whether this is because he is strong, or because he is too weak to face up to his own and other people's emotions.

Chapter 32

Jane becomes accepted in the village and finds her job better than it was at first. Although life seems tranquil, she is still plagued by disturbing dreams of Rochester. She is curious about the relationship between Miss Oliver and St John Rivers. She knows that Miss

Oliver and her father are in favour of a match and cannot understand why St John does not marry Miss Oliver. He will admit to only superficial regard for her and claims that she would not make him a suitable wife. He wants to serve God as a missionary and thinks that this will guarantee him a place in Heaven. As he leaves, St John tears a corner off a piece of paper which Jane has been using to draw on. He gives no explanation for doing this.

'I felt I became a favourite...'

Social class

Jane is happy to be warmly welcomed in the village, although she is conscious of her social position. But her contentment is only partial, as you can tell from the everyday expressions used to describe it: 'thankfulness', 'honourable', 'calm', 'useful'. Her true feelings and nature are revealed in her restless dreams which are 'agitating', 'exciting', 'force and fire'.

'Rosamond Oliver kept her word...'

St John continues to fight his love for Miss Oliver, not only because his heart

Love and passion

is dedicated to another cause, but also because his restless spirit would feel cramped by normal domestic life.

Although she is attractive, St John knows Miss Oliver would not make a suitable wife for him. Read the text carefully in order to find out what St John's attraction is for Miss Oliver and for Jane.

' "Is this portrait like?" '

Jane is perplexed by St John's continual denial of his feelings for Miss Oliver and she is determined to make him talk to her about it. He has not experienced Jane's direct way of talking to people before, and is taken aback by it, but he seems almost relieved to talk about Miss Oliver. Notice how cleverly Brontë uses a piece of behaviour to demonstrate the way he keeps control of his feelings: he takes out his watch in order to measure the time he will allow himself to speak.

' "It is strange", pursued he...'

St John Rivers

St John says he has indulged his feelings for Rosamond, but thinks they are essentially a 'delusion'. There is no place for her in his plans, because she will never make a missionary's wife. He sees his plans to be a missionary as his means of salvation: 'his foundation laid on earth'.

'I smiled incredulously.'

St John insists that he is driven by principle, not by emotion. Certainly he

does show himself to be cold, hard, determined and someone with affection only for his own family. He thinks of Jane only as 'a specimen of a diligent, orderly, energetic woman'. He seems to have no emotional feelings for her and to believe that religion must shape all the different aspects of a person's life. For him, love (or 'natural affection') must be turned into a dispassionate love for all mankind. He feels that his desire for power and leadership must be channelled into the life of a missionary, and that the job of religion is that of 'pruning and training nature'.

Love and passion

This attitude towards religion is very similar to the one Jane encountered at Lowood. She does not agree with it now any more than she did then.

Chapter 33

Jane hears of the fortune she has inherited and of her link with the Rivers family. She is glad of the independence her inheritance will bring her, but even more thrilled to know she has cousins – a real family. With difficulty, she persuades each of the others to accept a quarter of her fortune.

'Here was a new card turned up!'

The money will bring Jane independence. She seems to have little concern for the social advancement which such a large inheritance could bring. Jane

is more delighted with gaining a family than inheriting a fortune.

She wants to share her fortune four ways, because she thinks that the money is not really hers in 'justice', even if it is so in 'law'. She is more interested in the spirit of the law

Independence

than its letter. As she says a little later on: 'With me…it is fully as much a matter of feeling as of conscience: I must indulge my feelings…'.

Education

Though it is not over-stressed, Jane's work in teaching Adele and now in the village school balances the negative views of education at Lowood. Note that her sense of duty has warmed into feelings of pride and satisfaction by the time the school closes at the start of Chapter 34.

Chapter 34

Jane shuts the school and prepares Moor House for the return of Diana and Mary. St John disapproves because Jane seems to have nothing better to do than domestic chores. He is impatient to begin life as a missionary. Jane finds herself slipping increasingly under the influence of St John, who asks her to be his wife, even though he does not love her. She offers to go to India with him as his 'sister' but refuses to marry him, because she does not love him.

' "Doubtless." '

Jane has a strong need for personal fulfilment. It is not enough for her to spend

Jane Eyre

'a life devoted to the task'. St John advises her to look somewhere beyond this world for fulfilment, just as Helen Burns did. But Jane has always been the kind of person who wants to find 'the scene of fruition' in this world. St John has an overwhelming sense of self-righteousness. He warns Jane about 'selfish calm and sensual comfort' and reminds her that

it is her duty to God to use her talents to the full, not waste time on 'commonplace home pleasures'. She dismisses his preaching abruptly, because she feels that she can judge for herself whether or not she is wasting her talents on unworthy pursuits.

' "Tell him I will go." '

It is obvious that St John is uneasy with domestic life. He is much happier to be called out, even on the coldest night, because he can then feel fulfilled through doing his duty.

'I found him very patient...'

Jane is starting to submit to St John's will. She has already adjusted her

St John Rivers

behaviour to avoid his disapproval, and now she takes up 'Hindostanee', not because she wants to, but because he was 'not a man to be lightly refused'. Notice how this differs from the way she behaved when she was with Mr Rochester.

Look how Jane feels when St John gives her a goodnight kiss. To Jane the kiss seems 'a seal affixed to my fetters'. In her

relationship with St John, Jane has to suppress part of her personality. He tries to mould her.

Notice the imagery of coldness. Jane talks of coming under a 'freezing spell'. It is her own personality and independence that is becoming 'frozen' although you may guess that she will eventually rebel against this.

'St John called me to his side...'

Notice how far from her true self Jane has now come. In the past, her natural spirit has always been strong enough to fight back, but now she defers to every decision St John makes. Look at how detached he is as he watches her cry – there is no sympathy or comfort.

'I know no medium...'

Jane explains why she is behaving in this uncharacteristic way. She does not rebel yet, because she has still to reach 'the very moment of bursting', although you can tell that this moment is approaching.

' "And what does *your* heart say?" '

How different this is from Rochester's marriage proposal! For St John it would be solely a marriage of convenience, based on his idea that Jane would be a hard worker because she was 'formed for labour, not for love'. Clearly he does not know much about Jane's real character.

Jane has always relied on her instincts to help her to decide

Independence   what to do, but now they will not tell her whether this is the correct path to follow. Her use of the word 'fettered' reinforces that she is being 'enslaved' again.

Examiner's tip

St. John's proposal is another crucial scene. It is not only very revealing of his character, but pushes to extremes the theme of duty. Jane is loved only for what she can do: 'not personal, but mental endowments ... you are formed for labour, not for love.'

' "I am ready to go to India..." '

Read carefully the reasons Jane gives for reaching this decision. She is prepared

to go with him because she has found a way to fill the void left by Rochester without becoming St John's wife.

A marriage without love would be a lie for Jane and so she can only go to India as his sister and not as his wife. She sees that all St John – as 'the missionary' – wants is her 'energies',

Love and passion   not her 'self', and his denial of this, hiding behind God's name ('Do you think God will be sacrificed...') prompts her spirit to recover a little.

'I will not swear, reader...'

This is an important moment for Jane. She sees St John as an ordinary human being, with faults as well as virtues. This helps her gain confidence ('I was with an equal') and to be more like her old self. The spell she was under has been broken. From now on, she is able to distinguish 'the Christian'

Jane Eyre   from the man.

Love and passion

Jane knows she could put up with being St John's companion because there would be enough distance between them for her still to feel free in 'heart and mind'. But she cannot marry without love, 'forced to keep the fire of my nature continually low'. Her forthright manner has returned, because she has found her true nature again.

' "Then shake hands," I added.'

St John Rivers

Up to now, Jane has been unable to resist the demands of St John the Christian, but now that she can distinguish him from St John the man, she has no trouble in standing up to this part of him. St John the man is offended and refuses to say goodnight, but St John the Christian patiently suffers the blow to his pride.

Chapter 35

St John behaves coldly towards Jane because he cannot understand why she will not marry him and thinks she is wrong. Diana agrees that Jane and St John are unsuited. St John continues to put pressure on Jane and she begins to weaken. Jane agrees to marry St John if it is God's will, but then she hears Rochester's voice calling her name.

'He did not abstain from conversing...'

It is important to note that St John is not a very good example of the Christian notion of forgiveness. He says he has forgiven Jane but he cannot forget. His

St John Rivers

behaviour towards her is as cold and hard as marble. Jane describes him as: 'no longer flesh'. It is clear that his coldness would freeze her spirit. She tries very hard to appease St John, but he finds himself unable to reciprocate. He quotes the Gospel well enough, yet does not follow its precepts.

'A female curate, who is not...'

St John tries to make Jane feel guilty by talking about 'the dishonour' of

Jane Eyre

breaking her promise to him. But this fails, because Jane now has a clearer view of the kind of person he is. She is guided by common sense, whereas he is motivated by religious principle. He believes in self-sacrifice, whilst she sees no point in it at all. Jane's instinct for survival has carried her through all the difficult times in her life and there is another strong force that compels her to stay in England. St John does not understand the love between her and Rochester, calling it 'lawless and unconsecrated'. For St John, everything must be ruled by laws and principles.

' "I could decide if I were but certain..." '

You must be clear about what Jane has agreed to here. She agrees to submit to *God's* will – not St John's. She is desperate to do the right thing, but is struggling with herself – look at how she says: 'I contended with my inward dimness of vision...'.

'All the house was still...'

It is at this key moment, after Jane has asked heaven for help and guidance, that she hears within her the urgent supernatural voice of Rochester crying out her name 'in pain and woe'.

Jane's sense of God and of the supernatural are both linked to nature. Her feelings of right and wrong are based on what she feels is 'natural'. It is only now that she has fully worked this out. She has had to reject the laws she has been taught in the name of religion. She has found her own God now – see the section starting: 'I seemed to penetrate very near a Mighty Spirit...' – and she knows what it is right for her to do.

Nature and character

Chapter 36

Jane decides to return to Thornfield to discover what has happened to Rochester. When she gets there she finds it a blackened ruin. At the inn she learns that it was Bertha who set fire to the house and died in the flames. She also learns that Rochester was blinded and maimed in the fire, and now lives at Ferndean, his other home.

' "My spirit," I answered...'

Jane knows that she is doing the right thing but must still find how to go about

it. She is ready to 'search – enquire...', not just for Mr Rochester but also for certainty. You can tell that she thinks the two are linked.

She feels that Rochester's voice – whether real or imagined – has had a liberating effect on her mind. It has shown her the right path to follow.

Dreams

Note that Jane's dream in Chapter 25 'comes true' in the description of the burning down of Thornfield Hall.

Romance and mystery

An extended paragraph-long 'illustration' delays the moment when Jane tells of seeing the 'blackened ruin'. Du Maurier finds similar tension in *Rebecca* when the sunrise proves to be the blazing house (in both the house is a symbol as well as a building). Now the mystery can end as the innkeeper completes the story of **Bertha**.

Chapter 37

Jane goes to Ferndean and sees the blind Rochester in the garden. She watches him. He seems sullen and brooding. She goes to see him unannounced and tells him of her new-found financial independence. Their relationship blossoms again, but differently from before. She is now the one who teases him and makes him jealous. He has been humbled by his misfortune and is now more dependent on Jane so that the relationship between them is more equal. He wants to marry her without fuss or finery. He has begun to see the hand of God in all things.

'To this house I came...'

Environment

When Jane arrives at Ferndean, the weather matches her mood. Ferndean is hidden away and surrounded by dark woods, suggesting the state of Rochester's mind. Look at the way Brontë uses the elements – the weather changes the next day, along with Rochester's mood: 'The rain is over and gone...'

' "Which I never will, sir..." '

Jane Eyre

Already you can detect a change in their relationship. In the past it would never have been Jane who was the first to make her intentions clear. Notice the lighthearted way in which she speaks.

Rochester thinks that she will not want to marry him now that he has lost everything and been disfigured. Notice how Jane is now at 'perfect ease', her 'whole nature' having been 'brought to life and light' – so different from when she was with St John. This is her ideal of love.

' "It is a bright, sunny morning, sir..." '

Birds

Bird imagery is used to describe both of them. The pleasure of hearing her voice makes Rochester liken her to a skylark. He is still the chained 'eagle', now dependent on a mere 'sparrow'. His new dependence on her signals an equality between them which was not present before.

'Divine justice pursued its course'

Rochester begins to see the workings of God behind his troubles – in this way he is a better man for having to suffer blindness and mutilation. He is now on a more equal footing with Jane.

Chapter 38

All the loose ends are tidied up. We hear what happens to Adèle, to Mary and Diana, and to St John. Finally we learn that Jane and Rochester are very happy in their marriage and that his eyesight is partially restored.

'As to St John Rivers...'

St John becomes a missionary in India, converting the natives, clearing 'their painful way to improvement', while at the same time ensuring himself 'a place in the first rank...'. Notice the contrast between the attitude of St John to God and Mr Rochester's acceptance and humility through misfortune. Rochester seeks salvation through love. While Brontë promotes the idea that the way to God and true happiness is through love, not through wilful self-sacrifice and loveless duty, you should remember that St John is the ideal model of the Christian missionary, and does embody the virtues of self-sacrifice and duty: the novel ends with the anticipation of his death in God's services.

■ Self-test questions Chapters 27–38 (Volume 3)

Uncover the plot

Delete two of the three alternatives given, to find the correct plot. Beware possible misconceptions and muddles.

Jane resolves to stay/die/leave. Rochester says his father/ brother/partner tricked him: he 'could and ought' to kill Bertha/remarry/divorce. He asks Jane to go to France/Madeira/Ferndean as his 'wife/mistress/servant'. Only 'laws and principles/conscience/ feelings', enable her to leave – with a blessing/curse/silence. Left at Marsh End/Ferndean/Whitcross, Jane sleeps in town/moorland/churches and has to beg/work/steal for food. She follows a path/light/bell to Moor/Morton/ Marsh House where she recovers.

Mary and Hannah/Rosamund/Diana Rivers are soulmates; St John is overworked/content/confined as parson. Their uncle Robert/Edward/John has died. Jane becomes a schoolmistress/governess/seamstress in Morton. St John will be a missionary/artist/politician, leaving Diana/ Rosalind/Rosamund Oliver. Finding Jane's name is Eyre/Elliott/Reed, he says Eyre left her 20/5/1 thousand pounds – and the Rivers are her siblings/cousins/friends. Jane shares the money, and moves in with Diana and Mary/St John/Hannah. St John starts to ignore/love/dominate Jane, and calls her to join him in Madeira/ France/India: 'for labour/life/God, not for love'. Jane will go as his sister/wife/servant: he wants a wife/ curate/mistress. Jane is saved by St John's/God's/Rochester's voice. She finds Thornfield/Ferndean/ Gateshead a ruin. Bertha/Grace/Mrs Fairfax is dead, and Rochester blind/dead/ abroad. She finds him at Ferndean/London/Whitcross, and they are reunited and married. Rochester regains/loses/misses his sight.

Who? What? Why? How?

1   Who are the only two people at Thornfield who knew for certain about Bertha, and who suspected?

2   Who does the destitute Jane feel that she has a right to seek shelter from - and how does this turn out?
3   What hints do we get that the Rivers may be related to Jane, and how is this confirmed?
4   What happened at Thornfield after Jane's departure?
5   What insights does Jane gain into the nature and effects of poverty?
6   Why does St John want Jane to marry him, and why will she not do so?
7   Why does Jane think St John should marry Rosamund, and why will he not do so?
8   How and why was Rochester 'trapped' into marrying Bertha?
9   How does the story turn out for (a) Diana and Mary, (b) Adèle and (c) St John?
10 How has Rochester come to terms with his past, finally?

Mirror images
1   How do Jane and Rosamund sum up each other's character?
2   How is the 'kinship' between Jane and the Rivers sisters shown?
3   Give THREE examples of ways in which Diana and Mary differ from their brother.
4   Give TWO examples of how Jane and St John are (a) alike and (b) different.
5   Suggest TWO ways in which the 'new' Rochester is markedly different from the 'old'.
6   What is the greatness, and what the horror of St John's character, for Jane?

Two good men?
The central mirror image of the novel is Rochester and St John. What is the 'reverse image' of the following? (The numbers in brackets refer to chapters in which the comments on St John can be found.)
1   St John is like an 'Apollo': handsome and golden (37)
2   St John 'curbs vivacity' in Jane and his sisters (34), and doesn't respond to teasing
3   St John believes in sacrifice, life 'where courage is proved... energy exercised... fortitude tasked' (34)
4   St John 'could not bind all that he had in his nature... in the limits of a single passion' (32)
5   St John curbs his heart with 'despotic constriction'(31); calls himself 'a cold, hard man' (32)
6   St John's kiss is an 'experiment', a 'seal affixed to [Jane's] fetters' (34)
7   St John is 'reserved', unfailingly but coldly polite, even when crossed (35)
8   St John makes Jane 'disown her nature', 'stifle her faculties'. He is dominant, even 'despotic' (34)
9   St John's eyes 'search other people's thoughts' but do not 'reveal his own' (29)
10 St John speaks for God, as God's agent. 'If you reject it, it is not me you deny, but God' (34)

Who's boss?
The themes of rebellion and dependence centre on the 'triangle' of Jane, Rochester and St John. Let's explore... (The numbers in brackets refer to chapters where the answers can be found.)
1   What balance of power does St John envisage in the husband-wife relationship (34) – and what balance do Jane and Rochester find (37)?
2   Give FIVE examples of images associated with St John's 'ascendancy' or power over Jane (34, 35)
3   What is the final temptation for Jane to agree to marry St John, and what enables her to break free (35)?

How to write a coursework essay

Most of you are probably studying *Jane Eyre* as part of a Wide Reading coursework assignment for GCSE English/English Literature. If we look at the requirement of the NEAB examinations, we find that this assignment must involve *comparison* between a complete pre-twentieth-century prose text and a suitable twentieth-century text. It is also essential to make certain comments on the historical, social and cultural background to the texts. Such elements of *Jane Eyre* as nineteenth-century views on education and the role of women would be appropriate for this. In the following pages we examine three possible subjects for Wide Reading assignments. Throughout the **Text commentary** the **Essays icon** draws attention to useful material for these assignments.

There are, of course, some general principles for these assignments: *comparison is essential.* No credit is given for telling the story of all or part of *Jane Eyre* and that of a twentieth-century story with a vaguely similar theme. It is essential that you show that, while Brontë's presentation of love or education or the quest for independence has a certain effect, your twentieth-century author affects the reader totally differently, in the same or in a partially similar way.

Though comparison is essential, it is not required that you devote an equal amount of your essay to each of the texts. Similarly, there is no requirement that your twentieth-century comparative text is another novel: short stories, plays and poems are acceptable, and the only restriction is that the text 'must be of sufficient substance and quality to merit serious study'.

Your choice of twentieth-century comparative text is important. There must be *specific* grounds for comparison. Your 20th century example can be different, even opposite, in effect from Brontë: using similar ideas differently is a good ground for comparison. In the case of *Jane Eyre* there is the unusual situation that a major twentieth-century novel, *Wide Sargasso Sea,* even uses elements of the same story-line for notably different effect.

The *most important consideration* in writing the essay is that it must develop an argument or explain a point of view consistently throughout. Choosing a title matters: if you write an essay simply on the subject of Love and Marriage or Education in the two texts, you are not directing yourself towards a specific comparison. The comparison should be made throughout the essay, not necessarily in the same sentence, but at least in adjacent paragraphs. Careful advance planning will aid you in organising your theme or argument: making notes on the material, putting these notes in order, then working through two or three drafts of the essay. Thus you should be able to make a decision on what each paragraph is about, as far as possible signalling that to the reader in the opening sentence, often called a *topic sentence* because it states the topic of the paragraph.

In terms of length of essay, do bear in mind that it is only one of several pieces of coursework and there is no need for a 5,000 word blockbuster. Many essays will exceed 1,000 words: by how much depends on the material you wish to present and the advice of your teacher.

Bertha/Antoinette

What impression does Charlotte Brontë give of the character, behaviour and background of Mr Rochester's wife, Bertha? How does Jean Rhys use this material to create the character and story of Antoinette Cosway in Wide Sargasso Sea*?*

This is a difficult and challenging title which will require diligent and intelligent research through both novels, but could lead to an original and stimulating essay of a high standard. Jean Rhys, who wrote *Wide Sargasso Sea* (of which there have been several paperback editions) in 1966, was born in the Windward Islands of mixed Welsh and Creole parentage; not surprisingly, though the novel ends in Thornfield Hall, it emphasises West Indian character and beliefs.

In Chapter 26 of *Jane Eyre* Bertha's name is given as 'Bertha Antoinetta Mason', daughter of 'Jonas Mason, merchant' and his Creole wife. Jean Rhys takes the prettier second name and tells the story of Antoinette Cosway whose ruined and crazed mother re-marries the English merchant, Mr Mason. Mr Rochester, whose marriage to her is arranged, at first thinks her to be Mason's daughter. The three parts of the novel are: Antoinette's disturbed narrative of early years; Mr Rochester's account of a disastrous marriage; Antoinette's fractured memories of life locked up at Thornfield (as Bertha), ending with her leaving her room armed with a lighted candle.

It is important that you have a clear plan to keep control of such diverse material: you should start by examining Brontë's approach to the character of Bertha. She is not really seen in human terms. She is a main part of the 'Gothic' elements of the novel (all the wild sounds and mysterious deeds); she is part of Rochester's shadily romantic past; above all, she is a barrier to Jane and Rochester's quest for happiness. When she dies, the reader feels that the happy ending is now possible. No wonder Rhys wishes to give an identity to 'the madwoman in the attic' and tell the untold story.

You will need to see how the two novels interlock: examine the brief accounts of Rochester's first marriage given in *Jane Eyre* and see how Rhys uses them, especially in Part 2 of *Wide Sargasso Sea*, and compare Part 3 with Brontë's account of what Bertha does at Thornfield.

You are then ready to consider what Jean Rhys adds: her Antoinette has a disturbed and disturbing individuality, alienated certainly, but not the savage, inhuman animal of *Jane Eyre*. A comparison with Jane Eyre herself will find far more contrasts than similarities, but their situations have much in common (potential poverty, uncertain background, reliance on relatives by marriage), though the contrast between Gateshead and Coulibri Estate could not be greater!

There are many other themes and images where you could make valid comparisons between the two novels: the role of the outsider, the power of dreams, fire and destruction, the terrors of education, the challenge to masculine authority, etc. These are well worth considering on your way to a conclusion that should, in the case of this essay, be very much a personal response.

Education

Discuss the nature of Charlotte Brontë's views on education as presented in Jane Eyre. *Compare her criticisms of nineteenth-century education with a twentieth-century view, such as Barry Hines'* in A Kestrel for a Knave.

This is a straightforward essay where you should be careful to explain, not just give facts. As the title above hints, there are many alternatives to *A Kestrel for a Knave* as there is much twentieth-century fiction on the subject of the failures of education: just beware of so-called 'school stories' that fail the GCSE quality control. We will examine *A Kestrel for a Knave* to show how totally different books can be valid comparisons in *one specific area*.

Perhaps you should first clear out of the way some differences, some of which are too obvious to mention. However, three are worth noting. *Jane Eyre* belongs to an era when education for all did not exist: the Lowood pupils were supposedly the lucky ones! In *A Kestrel for a Knave* school is a part of daily life. The difference between boarding and day school should be noted. Finally, you should explain that comparison between the main characters (except as victims with undeveloped potential) is not a part of your intention.

You will then find surprising similarities and interesting differences which can be taken in any order you wish. You will want to contrast the principles of privation at Lowood with the casual neglect at Billy's school: it is a matter of principle to Brocklehurst that the girls should be half-starved, while the failings of the school in *A Kestrel for a Knave* are mostly the result of weariness and lack of interest. You will find neat comparisons of physical cruelty and public humiliation: Jane on a stool and Billy in huge shorts have to be compared! You can explain that both authors are concerned with the need for young people to be encouraged to develop their individual talents (both also show pointless lessons). You might enjoy contrasting Brocklehurst's bombast with Gryce's: neither has any respect for the pupils, Lowood's charity girls and the lads from the estate being equally powerless in economic and financial terms.

Equally, both books find positive signs where individuality and personal values are encouraged. In *A Kestrel for a Knave* this is found only in Farthing, unless you consider what Billy learns from Kes. There is much more of a positive approach to education in *Jane Eyre*: Miss Temple (a worthwhile comparison to Farthing – very different character, similar role), Helen's scholarship and goodness, the improved Lowood (very briefly) and Jane's teaching of Adele and the village children. You should ultimately be able to show that both books share views on what is important in education and show what can be achieved by a despised pupil.

Romance and mystery

How much of the success of Jane Eyre *as a novel depends upon Charlotte Brontë's use of romance and mystery? Compare her themes and methods with those of Daphne du Maurier in* Rebecca.

Where *Wide Sargasso Sea* deliberately tells the untold tale in *Jane Eyre*, Rebecca has no such openly admitted link, but, if you write on this assignment title, you will enjoy finding numerous connections of theme and detail between the two books: du Maurier's knowledge of Brontë is frequently apparent.

First of all, you need to think about those terms 'romance' and 'mystery'. *Jane Eyre* possesses many of the narrative features of the so-called 'romantic novel': after all, a poor, despised, plain girl marries a rich gentleman with a past and inherits a fortune on her own account. Apart from this, however, you need to examine other romantic elements: the spiritual response to nature, the use of dreams, the voyage of spiritual discovery, plus, of course, the use of mystery. Mystery is not confined to the first Mrs Rochester, though that particular mystery looms over the entire middle section of the novel: there are other mysteries of Rochester's past, mysteries of Jane's relations, mysteries of relationships (Rochester's deception over marriage to Blanche Ingram, the supernatural communication between Rochester and Jane, etc).

There is, of course, a moral dimension to *Jane Eyre* which is not present in *Rebecca*, but you will find that the use of romance and mystery provide many rewarding comparisons which you can arrange as you wish. A good starting point might be the use of the fire: the destruction of Manderley, as Thornfield, is anticipated (in dreams or recollections) much earlier, destroys the pride and independence of the wounded (physically/emotionally) husband and leads to a kind of shaken contentment in marriage. Or you could start with the heroine: Jane is cut off from family and possible wealth, du Maurier's character does not even have a name. One is working as a governess, one as a companion, when each meets a rich man troubled by past suffering who finds the solace in her love that he has previously sought in travelling Europe.

Opportunities then present themselves for comparing the two heroines: similarities (e.g. unease in rich company) and differences (e.g. Jane's greater independence and intelligence). Both share an identity problem: are they entitled to be wives? In each case a dramatic scene concerns an attempt to usurp the position of the first wife: at the Manderley Ball and at the failed marriage service. The first wife comparison will occupy several paragraphs: they are very different figures (Mrs Danvers takes part of the Bertha Mason role), but each creates mystery and foreboding and a major plot surprise. The mystery of the secret places in the house occurs in both novels. There are many other features which you could compare, from the use of dreams to the importance of the first person narrative.

Finally, the romance leads to a quiet retired marriage: Jane, at the end has been married peacefully and happily for ten years; the De Winters retreat into an exile punctuated by Test Match scores. Of course, *Jane Eyre* places this at the end of the characters' moral progress; *Rebecca*, a more melodramatic novel, is arranged so that the burning of Manderley is the last thing we read.

▪ How to write an examination essay

Though most of you will be required to write on *Jane Eyre* as part of your coursework, some of you may need to answer an examination question on it. This section considers one specific title on the novel, but also gives general advice on how to approach an English Literature essay.

Jane Eyre receives two proposals of marriage in the course of the novel. Give accounts of the characters of Mr Rochester and St. John Rivers, comparing their relationships with Jane. You should consider such things as:

- *what their feelings are for her;*
- *what they hope for in marriage;*
- *what emotions they inspire in her.*

Before you start writing

- The first essential is thorough revision. It is important that you realise that even Open Book examinations require close textual knowledge. You will have time to look up quotations and references, but *only if you know where to look.*

- Read the questions very carefully, both to choose the best one and to take note of exactly what you are asked to do.

- Do not answer the question you *imagine or hope* has been set. In the case of the title we are considering, you are not asked to tell the stories of the two courtships and proposals. You are asked to *compare* the two men, especially in their relationships with Jane. Therefore you will need to contrast warmth with coldness, joy in the present with a carefully planned future (with a working role for Jane), awareness and disregard for Jane as a person, as well as a more general contrast of the passionate and humorous man of substance with the obsessively dedicated missionary-to-be. You are specifically asked to comment on Jane's feelings and must do so.

- Identify all the key words in the question that mention characters, events and themes, and instructions as to what to do, e.g. compare, contrast, comment, give an account, etc. Write a short list of the things you have to do. In this case 'give an account' requires a sound summary of their characters and 'compare' requires such phrasing as 'Whereas Rochester ..., St. John Rivers, on the other hand ...'

- Look at the points you have identified and jot down what you are going to say about each. Decide in what order you are going to deal with the main points. Number them in sequence. This is a matter of choice, but do not use chronological order: 'Jane first meets Rochester when he sprains his ankle in a fall from his horse.' You may wish to give an account of Rochester, followed by one of Rivers, before moving on to comparisons and a consideration of the two courtships. This is perfectly acceptable, so long as your accounts of character are just that, not accounts of what they do.

Writing the essay

- The first sentences are important. Try to summarise your response to the question so the examiner has some idea of how you plan to approach it. For example: 'The two most prominent male characters in *Jane Eyre*, Mr Rochester and St. John Rivers, present opposites both in terms of character and in terms of the alternative views of life between which Jane must choose.' Jump straight into the essay; do not nibble at the edges for a page and a half. A personal response is rewarded, but you must always answer the question – as you write your essay, *refer back* to your list of points.

- Answer *all* of the question. Many students spend all their time answering just one part of a question and ignoring the rest. This prevents you gaining marks for the parts left out. In the same way, failing to answer enough questions on the examination is a waste of marks which can always be gained most easily at the start of an answer.

- There is no 'correct' length for an essay. What you must do is to spend the full time usefully in answering all parts of the question: spending longer than the allocated time by more than a few minutes is dangerous. It is an advantage if you can organise your time so well as to reach an elegant conclusion (perhaps summarising why Jane makes the choice she does), but it is better to leave an essay without a conclusion than to fail to start the next question.

- Take care with presentation, spelling and punctuation. It is generally unwise to use slang or contractions (e.g. 'they've' for 'they have').

- Use quotation or paraphrase when it is relevant and contributes to the quality and clarity of your answer. References to events often do not need quotation, but the exact words of, for instance, recurring imagery such as the coldness and hardness of St. John Rivers are needed to prove Brontë's intention. *Extended* quotations are usually unhelpful and are often used as padding, which is a complete waste of time.

■ Self-test answers Chapters 1–15 (Volume 1)

Uncover the plot

Jane lives with Mrs Reed at Gateshead Hall: even the nurse Bessie calls her 'less than a servant'. Fighting John Reed, she is locked in the red-room, and has a fit. An apothecary suggests a school. Mr Brocklehurst accepts her for Lowood school, where her first breakfast is burnt porridge. She meets Helen Burns, who patiently suffers the injustices of Miss Scatcherd, and sustains Jane when Mr Brocklehurst 'exposes' her as a liar. Jane also loves the superintendent Miss Temple. One spring, the school is hit by typhus: Helen dies of consumption. Later, when Jane is a teacher, Miss Temple marries and Jane leaves to be a governess.

At Thornfield, Jane is welcomed by Mrs Fairfax, the house-keeper, and her pupil Adèle. On the third floor, she hears a laugh: Grace Poole? One still day, Jane meets Rochester when his horse falls. Conversations follow: about Jane and her paintings, and about Rochester – his hopes of reformation, and his betrayal by Celine. Jane saves Rochester from a fire.

Who? What? Why? How?

1   Mr Eyre, a poor clergyman, who died of typhus while visiting the poor. Mrs Reed dismisses the family as 'beggarly' (3) but Bessie reports that Mr Eyre's brother 'looked quite a gentleman' (10)
2   Gateshead: Bessie and Mr Lloyd, the apothecary. Lowood: Helen Burns and Miss Temple
3   Being locked in the red-room: resistence, humiliation, horror, depression (2) Being made to stand on a stool in school: humiliation – but then courage and resignation, thanks to Helen (7)
4   Mr Brocklehurst's 'exposure' of Jane (7) Tea with Helen and Miss Temple (8) Helen's death (9)
5   (a) Jane is excited by learning and success (end 8). (b) Spring, freedom to roam outside the walls (9)
6   She refuses to idolise children as some do (12). She learns that Adele is a fellow 'orphan'. (15)
7   Miss Temple is gone: Jane wants to escape. 'Liberty' and 'change, stimulus' are too much to ask: 'a new servitude' is allowable (10)
8   Mrs Reed is scared, by the truth – or by Jane's threat to tell everyone. Jane is driven to fight back by the injustice of Mrs Reed's claim that she is 'deceitful', poisoning her future with Brocklehurst (4)
9   The bigger girls take their meagre food rations, and exclude them from the warmth of the fire (7)
10 To keep the pupils 'humble' and 'to render them hardy, patient, self-denying' (7)

Mirror images

1   Jane says she'd 'strike back' against unjust punishment (6) and does – mentally or physically (4, 8)
2   Jane says: 'I must dislike those who... persist in disliking me' (6)
3   Jane fears death: in the red-room (2) and at Lowood: ('an unfathomed gulf') (9)
4   Jane clings to self-respect: 'if others don't love me, I would rather die than live' (8)

5   Helen's 'natural' faith contrasts with Jane's doubt (9) and the hard religiosity of Brocklehurst (7)

Looking forward to it?
1   The hints become increasingly ominous and Helen finally dies of consumption (9)
2   Bessie brings a different story (10). Later, we find that Mr Eyre is rich, and Jane has other family (33)
3   Jane will visit the dying Mrs Reed, 'yearning to forget and forgive' and calling her 'dear aunt' (21)
4   First impressions confirm this (11) – but Thornfield later turns out to be anything but orderly!

Familiar themes
1   (a) Stone and architecture, 'black marble' (4, 7) (b) Light in the darkness (we first see her carrying a lamp; light shines from her room), and food (she organises extra meals, gives Jane and Helen tea) (8)
2   Bewick's History of British Birds, Goldsmith's History of Rome (1), Gulliver's Travels (3), Arabian Nights, the Bible (4). (a) Ballads and novels like Pamela (1) (b) Rasselas, by Dr Johnson (5)
3   Comfort – light and warmth in the hearth. Passion – as in Jane's image of the forest fire after her battle with Mrs Reed (4). Thornfield is later burnt to the ground – passion leading to both ruin and liberation
4   Examples include: 'resisted', 'mutiny', 'rebel slave' (1st paragraph), 'escape', 'insurrection', 'battle'
5   (a) John's character, too, is coarse and ugly (1); (b) Jane feels inferior in her plainness (3, 10). Note how she hates people looking at her (7); (c) The girls' curled hair exposes their father's hypocrisy (7)

The odd couple
1   Otherworldly setting. Destiny (Pilot) uniting them. His leaning on her – needing her despite his dominant manner. His roughness setting her at ease. Her courage and independence. (12)
2   Age and experience, though later (Chapter 20) he admits that he is 'heart-weary and soul-withered' where she is 'fresh and healthy'.
3   He sprains his ankle (12). Later he needs Jane's moral strength.
4   Imagination (13), ability to listen (15), honesty (15), purity of heart and mind (14).

◼ Self-test answers Chapters 16–26 (Volume 2)

Uncover the plot
After an absence of more than a fortnight, Rochester returns, bringing home a party, including Blanche Ingram.

Jane now loves Rochester, while believing he will marry Blanche. Rochester, disguised as a gypsy, shows strong feelings for Jane. After Mason is attacked, they walk in the garden. Rochester says only 'an obstacle of custom' keeps him from a new life – but his 'cure' is Blanche.

Jane visits a dying Mrs Reed: only Jane has changed. Returning, Jane meets Rochester in the lane. One evening, he talks of a post in Ireland – but then renounces Blanche, and proposes. Jane has nightmares, and is terrified by a madwoman. The wedding is stopped by Briggs, with Mason as witness. Rochester confesses: his wife Bertha is alive.

Who? What? Why? How?

1   Mrs Dent: 'less showy'; slight, pale, black-clad; likes flowers, 'especially wild ones', is kind to Adèle. (17)
2   Dowager Lady Ingram. (17)
3   She is 'very near happiness'. He wants 'smiles… endearments', but is restraining his emotions. (19)
4   Curls (remember the Brocklehurst girls). Elegant dress. Tall stature. Haughty expression. (17)
5   Eyre's letter to Mrs Reed, seeking to adopt Jane (21) and her reply (24), which alerts Eyre's friend Mason to her engagement – to his brother-in-law! (26)
6   Jane will not be losing Rochester to a better woman: Blanche will not win his love as she could. (18)
7   Mr Reed preferred his sister's child to his own. She can't see good in Jane without admitting guilt. (21)
8   21: neither she nor Adèle can live with Blanche; 23: she could not bear his (supposed) indifference; 26: lost confidence in him - and he won't want her now that his existing marriage is revealed.
9   Rochester's reaction to him is dramatic (19). His attack – on the third floor at night– is kept secret. He clearly knows his attacker. He has the power to injure Rochester with 'one careless word'. (20)
10 He talks of marrying Blanche, says he has a post for Jane in Ireland; she must leave for ever. (23)

Mirror images

1   No: an unflattering self-portrait in chalk, and an idealised portrait in oils (17)
2   Jane supports the right of women to find 'exercise for their faculties' (12). Blanche supports their right to exact homage for their beauty, dismissing the ugly woman as 'a blot on the fair face of creation' (17)
3   She is 'showy…not genuine': she has a 'barren' heart, with no spontaneity. She is not 'good', nor 'original', with no opinions of her own. She lacks 'tenderness and truth', 'sympathy and pity' (17)
4   He is 'handsome and amiable' – but lacks 'power', 'firmness', 'thought', 'command' (18)

Make the connection

1   (a) Mason is Bertha's brother. (b) Rochester is Bertha's husband. (c) Their fathers were friends (26)
2   (a) Mason convalesces in Madeira with Eyre – a colleague. (b) Jane writes to Eyre – her uncle – about her marriage. (26) Briggs serves to make the link, as he later (33) does in connecting the Rivers to Jane as cousins, the children of Eyre's sister.
3   Mrs Fairfax warns Jane (24); Jane ironically says: 'Mrs Rochester… didn't exist' (25); Rochester talks of judgement, defiance (24); The veil is torn in two (25)
4   Eyre will leave Jane money (26). The chestnut stays joined at the root (25). Rochester's strong hand and arm are 'a dream' (25). They will stand 'equal' after 'both had passed through the grave' (23)

Picture this!

1   Blanche's heart is 'soil' on which 'nothing bloomed spontaneously' (17). Mason affects Rochester like lightning hitting an oak. (20)
2   Rochester is like a 'rough-coated, keen-eyed dog' (18) - but there is 'snarling, canine noise' on the third floor. Jane is like a caged bird which would 'soar

cloud-high' and Rochester is a 'fierce falcon' (18) - but the madwoman's voice is that of a 'carrion-seeking bird of prey' (20). Bertha spoils the positive images.

3   On the night of horror, the moonlight is shut out of the third floor. Sunrise offers hope: Rochester 'lets in all the daylight he could' (20). Earlier moon and daylight cast an ambivalent light on the first meeting. (12)

Family fortunes

1   The house, Bessie and (partly) the Reeds are the same. Jane's attitude has changed. (21)

2   Mr Eyre tried to adopt her: Mrs Reed said she was dead. Jane writes - causing the crisis. (21, 26)

3   Thornfield is 'home'; she is Adèle's 'little English mother', and Mrs Fairfax's 'adopted' daughter. (22)

4   Jane accepts her past - forgiving and asking forgiveness - and so overcomes it (21). Rochester still 'carries' his past as a curse, but tries to defy its power over his future. (27)

▇ Self-test answers Chapters 27–38 (Volume 3)

Uncover the plot

Jane resolves to leave. Rochester says his father tricked him: he 'could and ought' to remarry. He asks Jane to go to France as his 'wife'. Only 'laws and principles' enable her to leave – with a blessing. Left at Whitcross, Jane sleeps in moorland and has to beg for food. She follows a light to Moor House where she recovers.

Mary and Diana Rivers are soulmates; St John is confined as parson. Their uncle John has died. Jane becomes a schoolmistress in Morton. St John will be a missionary, leaving Rosamund Oliver. Finding Jane's name is Eyre, he says Eyre left her 20 thousand pounds – and the Rivers are her cousins. Jane shares the money, and moves in with Diana and Mary. St John starts to dominate Jane, and calls her to join him in India: 'for labour, not for love'. Jane will go as his sister: he wants a wife. Jane is saved by Rochester's voice. She finds Thornfield a ruin. Bertha is dead, and Rochester blind. She finds him at Ferndean, and they are reunited and married. Rochester regains his sight.

What? Why? How?

1   Grace Poole and Doctor Carter. Mrs Fairfax suspected - hence her misgivings. (27)

2   The clergyman. He is away - but we soon suspect that St. John, who takes her in, is the same man. (28)

3   The wealthy 'uncle John', who has 'one other' relative (30). Briggs enquires after Jane Eyre – the heiress – and St John recognises the name scrawled on the corner of Jane's drawing pad (33)

4   Rochester sought her, 'grew savage', sent away Adèle and Mrs Fairfax, shut himself away. Bertha set fire to the house at night, jumped from the roof: Bertha, trying to save her, lost an eye and hand (36)

5   She says poverty is not a crime (29) but learns in Morton that 'the germs of... refinement, intelligence, kind feeling, are as likely to exist in [peasant] hearts as in those of the best-born' (31)

6   For her 'mental endowments': tact, calm, resolution, energy, courage, faithfulness (34) She knows he will never love her: she would be 'always restrained... always checked' (35)

7   They love each other, her father approves, her fortune will help him do good. She could not 'sympathize' with his aspirations, or 'co-operate' in his undertakings (32)

8. His father wanted him to have her fortune. Her nature, and mother's madness, were kept from him. (27)

9   Diana and Mary marry happily. Adèle is placed in a good school, and turns out well. St John follows his destiny to India: it is implied that he will die an early but glorious death (38)

10 He faces his sins and wrong decisions, accepts God's judgement, is reconciled and renewed (37)

Mirror images

1   Rosamund: 'coquettish... hasty... vain... unthinking... not profoundly interesting' Jane: 'good, clever, composed, and firm', like St John (32)

2   They share a love of nature, books and art. They are governesses, to provide for themselves (29)

3   They show 'compassion': he gives 'charity' (29). They offer to teach Jane German, he makes her learn Hindustani (34). He does not love nature as they do (30)

4   Alike in fighting the degrading temptation of passion (31). Alike in rebellion against confinement (32). But St John is cold, Jane hot (33). Jane is 'natural': St John has subdued nature (34)

5   He is dependent instead of dominant – and not too proud to admit it. He no longer defies God, but accepts His judgement and is reconciled (37)

6   He is a good man, 'firm, faithful, and devoted, full of energy and zeal, and truth' (38). He is cold, hard, ambitious, 'inexorable as death': 'pure as the deep sunless source' (35)

Two good men?

1   Rochester is like 'Vulcan', dark, elemental, blind and lame. (37)

2   Rochester brings out Jane's spirit – without 'harrassing restraint', and comes alive with her teasing (37)

3   Rochester believes in his right to be happy. 'I have little left in myself – I must have you' (37)

4   Rochester focuses all his passion on Jane: she is 'the alpha and omega of [his] heart's wishes' (37)

5   Rochester is passionate, almost violent, in love as in despair (27, 37)

6   Rochester's first kiss is passionate (23), his embrace on her return natural, heartfelt, vulnerable (37)

7   Rochester's 'harshness' and 'sarcasm' are full of passion, and add 'spice' to the relationship (18)

8   Rochester loves Jane's spirit; wants her for his equal: she is at her most independent with him (23, 27)

9   Rochester's eyes speak to Jane; even sightless, they move her; a symbol of how he give of himself (37)

10 Rochester, with natural spirituality, first defies then comes humbly to God, and is reconciled (37)

Who's boss?

1   He wants to 'influence efficiently in life, and retain absolutely till death' (34). Rochester accepts a dependent role; Jane loves him more than in his 'state of proud independence' (37)

2   A 'freezing spell'; an 'iron shroud'; a 'rayless dungeon' with a 'shrinking fear fettered in its depths'; an 'avalanche' (34); rushing down the 'torrent of his will into the gulf of his existence' (35)

3   Veneration of his zeal and earnestness, the influence of his gentleness, his appeal to her desire to do the right thing. She prays to be shown 'the path' – and hears Rochester's voice calling her (35)